# THE ULTIMATE
# HOUSE HACKING
## GUIDE FOR DENVER

*A TECHNICAL GUIDE TO BUILDING A DENVER RENTAL PORTFOLIO THROUGH HOUSE HACKING*

CHRIS LOPEZ, JOE MASSEY, JEFF WHITE

Published by:
Chris Lopez
2755 South Locust St #150
Denver, CO 80222
www.DenverInvestmentRealEstate.com

# Table of Contents

# Introduction

Many aspiring house hackers understand the concept and long-term wealth building potential of house hacking, but they lack the local knowledge on how to apply it to the Denver market. We wrote this book to provide the technical details of buying house hacks and building a rental portfolio here in Denver.

This is a collaborative effort of Chris Lopez, Joe Massey and Jeff White. The three of us share many common beliefs towards investing. You'll quickly notice that we have our differing points of view as well. Guess what? There is no one "right" way to invest. This statement is even more true with house hacking since you're balancing your personal living needs with an investment property. One of the goals of this guide is to educate you to help you figure out the "right" way for you.

The one downside of having three authors is keeping the voice of the book consistent. The book does bounce around between the first and third person voices. Chris took the lead on writing the book. When it reads in the first person, that is Chris. Please don't beat us up on it because none of us are professional writers. Other than that, the book came out better than our expectations.

# About the Authors

**Chris Lopez** is an Investor-friendly agent at Your Castle Real Estate. He helps investors build a rental portfolio through house hacking and buying traditional rental properties. He also helps investors create a real estate retirement plan to target a monthly cash flow in retirement. Chris is also an investor and is currently doing a multigenerational family house hack. You can reach Chris at 303-548-0846 or Chris@DenverInvestmentRealEstate.com.

**Joe Massey** is a Senior Loan Officer and Branch Manager at Castle & Cooke Mortgage. Joe helps house hackers, investors and homebuyers with getting the best permanent financing in place based on their situation and the property. Joe is an active investor. You can reach Joe at 303-809-7769 or jmassey@castlecookemortgage.com.

**Jeff White** is a house hacking coach who helps investors with maximizing their returns and stabilizing their properties. He's an active house hacker who is using this investing method to achieve financial independence. You can reach Jeff at 720-951-6868 or thehousehackingcoach@gmail.com.

If you have any questions, do not hesitate to reach out to us. We're always happy to chat about house hacking.

# House Hacking in Colorado Springs

While writing this book, a great opportunity popped up for Chris to partner with an agent in Colorado Springs. Her name is Jenny Bayless. She's an active investor in the Springs and a CPA turned investor-friendly Realtor. Long story short, we had just enough time to add a chapter on Colorado Springs to this book to highlight some of the differences. If you're interested in the Springs market, make sure you keep an eye on the Denver Real Estate Investing podcast and email list as Jenny and Chris will be doing a deep dive into the market!

Enjoy the book!

Chris, Joe & Jeff

# House Hacking Toolkit

Throughout the book, we'll reference a few spreadsheets and tools. If you want to download the spreadsheets to follow along, then download our House Hacking Toolkit for free.

Part of the toolkit is public to everyone, the rest is for clients only. A client is someone who is actively working with or has purchased a property with Chris Lopez and his team.

**The public toolkit includes:**

- Joe Massey's Denver Rental Property Analyzer Spreadsheet. Use this spreadsheet for analyzing individual properties.

- The house hacking modeling spreadsheet. Use this spreadsheet to run financial models for buying four properties.

- Deal analyses of closed house hacking transactions. See what active house hackers are buying in the Denver market!

- Investing classes, which include house hacking specific classes.

**The client toolkit includes:**

- A room-by-room lease that one of our lawyers drafted for our clients to use.

- Access to AirDNA.co rental comps. We have a state-wide license for Airdna.co to run rental comps. If you want Airbnb comps for a property, just email us.

- Coaching with Jeff White! We want to see you succeed after you close on the property. After closing, we're gifting you a coaching package with Jeff.

- Join one of our house hacking masterminds to meet and network with other active house hackers. The focus is beyond buying your first property and is about running your properties efficiently and building long term wealth.

Our clients also get access to all our of other client perks as well. Go to www.DenverInvestmentRealEstate.com/HHToolkit for all the details and to download the spreadsheets.

# Chapter 1

# House Hacking in the Denver Market

## What is House Hacking?

I believe BiggerPockets coined the term "house hacking." While it's a newer term and a great name that they coined, this investing strategy has been around for a long time. Here's how each of us define it:

My definition: "Buying a property that you'll live in while you're renting out part of it to reduce your living expenses or live for free."

Joe's definition: "Living in a property and renting out a portion of it. The portion you're renting out will generate rent for you that you can use to make mortgage payments and offset living expenses."

Jeff's definition: "House Hacking is purchasing a primary residence with a low down payment, renting out the other rooms or units to achieve the highest rental income to offset the mortgage costs, and aiming to live for free until the next property."

## House Hacking Variations

- Buy a duplex, triplex or fourplex; live in one unit and rent out the others.

- Buy a house, condo or townhouse; live in one room and rent out individual rooms.

- Use Airbnb or another service to rent out rooms or your property on a short-term basis. **Make sure to follow the rules!**

- Rent out the garage or RV parking pad for additional income.

- Have grandparents, parents and children all living in one property to save on living costs.

Ultimately, house hacking is a balancing act between your personal needs and your investing needs. Don't get hyper focused on one property type or one way to generate income. There is no right or wrong way as there are several different versions of house hacking; it's about what works best for your individual situation.

We've previously named Jeff White as the "poster child" for house hacking in Denver. Jeff has house hacked a fourplex, rented room by room and used Airbnb for short-term rentals.

I'm currently living in a variation of the multigenerational house hack. We converted the basement into its own living space for my mother-in-law. She helps with childcare and cooking meals. It's a great setup for a family and saves us over $2,000/mo.

# House Hacking vs. Traditional Investing

The number-one difference between house hacking and traditional investing is that you're going to live in the property. Lenders give much more favorable terms to people who are buying a house as their primary residence than an investor who is buying a rental property.

Let's say a person owns their primary residence and one rental property, then the economy hits a rough patch and he can only afford to pay one mortgage. Is he going to pay the mortgage on the house where his family lives or his rental property? Most likely, his primary residence. Lenders realize this and offer much more favorable lending terms.

The 4 main differences are:

- Down Payment - The down payment required for a primary residence can be as low as 0%-5%. For a traditional investment property, you typically need 15%-25%.

- Interest Rate - In general, the rates for a primary residence are significantly lower than they will be for any investment property.

- Primary Residence - You need to live in the property as a primary residence.

- One-Year Occupancy - It needs to be where you continue to reside for one year.

# Real-Life Example

I helped Jeff buy his third house hack property for $485,000. Joe helped Jeff with his loan. Jeff was buying as an owner-occupant. Joe was able to offer a more favorable interest rate and require less of a down payment from Jeff. When it came time for closing, Jeff was required to bring only $17,000 to the closing table. Lenders don't care if you're house hacking, they just care if it's your primary residence or not.

If I purchased the same $485,000 property as an investor, the lowest down payment would be $72,750 (15% * $485,000).

My down payment would be four times as much money! To keep it simple, the power of using owner-occupant financing is that you get to keep more money in your pocket. The added benefits gained from financing a house hack are overwhelming and are why the house hacking strategy is preferred over traditional investing if you are up for it.

| | Down Payment | Interest Rate | Primary Residence | One-Year Occupancy | Down payment on a $485k property |
|---|---|---|---|---|---|
| Jeff (house hacker) | 0%-5% | Lower | Required | Yes | $17,000 |
| Chris (investor) | 15%-25% | Higher | Not Required | No | $73,000 |

# House Hacking vs. Nomad™

If you start to gather information online about house hacking, it won't take you long to see that the common house hacking scenario described is one in which you buy a duplex or fourplex, live in one unit and rent out the other unit(s). However, those blog articles are usually not written by Denver house hackers! The current Denver market makes it so buying a multi-family unit is not always the best or easiest move. We'll discuss why in more detail in a later chapter.

Don't get fixated on finding the "grand slam" of a house hack. Let's say I wait for this best-case scenario and get my fourplex house hack. I'm living for free, and I'm cash-flowing about $1,000 per month from the rent I'm collecting. I've found this amazing property, so I decided to stay in it for 10 years.

At the same time, Jeff does the same thing but stays in his properties for the required one year. With the same timeline of 10 years, Jeff now owns 10 properties while I own one. In the long-term, who will be wealthier? Well it doesn't take a mathematician to know that income from 10 properties will beat income from one property.

The term we use to describe the process Jeff used in the example above is Nomading™. It's a term that was coined by our investor friend and Realtor in Fort Collins, James Orr. We use this term to help clients distinguish between traditional house hacking and the process of obtaining not just one property but the sequential process of buying multiple properties to build long-term wealth.

With Nomading™, you're buying and living in a future rental property. You may or may not house hack with tenants or roommates.

Again, using our poster child, Jeff, he first bought a fourplex, lived in it for one year, then bought a single-family home, lived there for a year, then bought his current house. He's combining traditional house hacking with the Nomad™ strategy to help expedite his accumulation of properties, which, in return, will accelerate his amount of wealth. Using the Nomad™ strategy to acquire and repeat is a powerful way of building your wealth through real estate.

Overall, you don't need to find the perfect house hack or that one "grand slam;" you need to find good, "base hit" house hacks.

Collecting those base hits over time builds the foundation and sets you up for long-term success.

It's changing your mindset to start thinking more long-term. Don't get stuck on finding something perfect today, but instead, think about what will make the most sense five, ten, or twenty years from now. The answer, to put it very simply, is owning multiple properties. In later chapters, we'll discuss examples in detail.

If you want to stack your returns, combine house hacking and the Nomad™ strategy like Jeff does.

**Note:** For simplicity's sake, I'll generally combine the investing strategies and just refer to house hacking throughout this book.

## What Strategy Is Right for You?

Our famous question, which we will continue to ask again and again through this series: Which method is right for you?

Our classic answer: It depends on your situation.

Are you single, no spouse and no kids? Does moving every one to two years, having roommates and managing a house with several people seem like a manageable task? If so, maybe you're like Jeff and house hacking is a great fit!

Are you married, have two kids and want to focus on how to best balance improving your quality of life while also creating ways to save on living expenses? Maybe you're more like me who is doing a multigenerational house hack, which is saving me over $2,000 per month. I live in a very unique situation. Many people cannot live with their family for numerous reasons. Many of my family clients focus solely on the Nomad™ strategy.

Maybe you're wanting to try a house hack but, as life's obligations of family and kids grow, you realize you want to stay in one house, so you switch your focus to a more traditional investment strategy.

Regardless of which strategy you choose or what modifications you apply, you have to make the decisions that are right for your individual situation. You have to be comfortable with your scenario and balance your priorities of investing with your quality of life. There is no clear-cut right or wrong answer. There is more to this than analyzing a property with a spreadsheet!

On paper we can make a case for both pros and cons of participating in house hacking or really any investing strategy. Ultimately, the important thing to remember is that with any investment strategy, house hacking included, your mindset will play a huge role in your success or failure of those investments.

Jeff illustrates a great example of exactly how his mindset sets him up to be successful, no matter the circumstances because, for every con we put on the list above, he came up with how that con could be looked at as a pro.

While moving every year to two years will seem daunting to most, if you have Jeff's point of view, you can see how moving every year forces you to be more efficient in material belongings and live a more minimalist lifestyle. When you don't have 4 tables, 3 couches, 2 TVs, multiple bed sets and boxes upon boxes of crap, suddenly, moving isn't as daunting of a task as it could be.

When you take the time to properly and effectively screen your tenants, there's less of a likelihood that you will end up with tenants who will cause issues. When you set expectations and house rules from day one, you set a standard for tenants to adhere to and hopefully cause less issues between roommates. We as humans also have a natural ability to easily adapt to most situations, so, once living with others becomes part of your new "normal" routine, it doesn't have to cause you the stress you might think.

With higher leverage and risk, it's good to remind yourself to think longer-term. House hacking allows for huge savings up front so you can increase your ability to save and accumulate properties quickly, but then allows you to have more options when the time for house hacking ends and you want to transition to a more traditional method of investing.

The great part about having Jeff as an expert in this series is we get to pull back the curtain and see exactly how Jeff does these things. In later chapters, we will get to see how Jeff screens his tenants, what expectations Jeff sets for those tenants and how he handles the day-to-day issues of living with other tenants.

# Common Questions

### How much money do I need to house hack?

When it comes to down payment and money needed to buy a house in the Denver market, be prepared to invest about 5% of the purchase price and around $5,000 in closing and acquisition costs. You can do it with less, but most of my clients end up investing between $20,000 and $35,000. You can do lower down payment loans such as FHA or VA, so make sure you talk with a lender to see what options you have.

## Does house hacking still work in the Denver market?

With prices going crazy and inventory being so low in the Denver market, it's easy to see why you would think this wouldn't be possible, however, it is. Jeff is just one example. There are still plenty of deals out there and ways to make house hacking work! It's about being able to think creatively, building the team of lenders and brokers who know the market, setting you up with good expectations and, ultimately, finding a property that works for your situation.

## What is the best property type? A multi-family, right?

Classic answer: It depends! Don't get hyper focused on one type of property. The best property type depends on your individual situation and several factors that may be out of your control. Continue on to chapter, *The Best Properties for House Hacking,* for more details.

## I don't want to live with tenants, what can I do?

You can focus on a property that has totally separate living quarters, such as a multi-family property or a house with separate entrances for a mother-in-law suite. Another option would be to focus on the Nomad™ strategy. It won't matter which house hack method you used because you would have several properties which are contributing to your wealth and investment goals. Investors who live with tenants are usually doing so to save money for a down payment on their next property.

If you don't want to live with tenants, you can also live in the property longer to save more, you can go out and create a side hustle to help increase your savings rate per month, or you can get creative and think about how your property can generate other forms of income—like renting out a garage or RV space.

My clients who are executing the Nomad™ strategy are families and couples who want more privacy and do need the house hacking income to save for the down payment on the next Nomad™ property.

## Should I flip or house hack?

This is definitely a loaded question and everyone will have a different point of view, but in general, flipping produces a short-term gain while house hacking produces a long-term gain. Flipping is a job or business. House hacking, after you move out, is more of a passive investment.

To be a good flipper, you have to have lots of skills and relationships to make things move quickly and smoothly. Flipping is a business, not a hobby. If you are a good flipper, (not a lot of people are) in the Denver market, you can expect between $20-$50k in short-term profits.

With house hacking, you are able to achieve comparable returns for much less work and you get to cash-in on that year after year. House hacking is more effective for long-term wealth. Another great thing about house hacking is that you can get the hands-on real estate and flipping experience without the risks of a flip by being a live-in landlord. You know what breaks down and how to fix it, and you gain some insight if you were to then do a flip.

We're not discouraging you from flipping, but many people spend years trying to do their first flip while renting a place. You can house hack at the same time to start building real estate retirement income. We get it, house hacking isn't sexy, nor does it throw up big dollar amounts like flipping, but it's a damn good way to start investing with very low risk.

## Can I BRRRR (Buy, Rehab, Renovate, Rent, Repeat) and house hack?

Sounds good on paper, but it's very hard to do in the Denver market. It's basically a unicorn scenario. Ultimately, numbers don't work because of how little down you get the house hack for. It is much more realistic to focus on house hacks which will build wealth instead of combining these two strategies. A big bonus with house hacking is that you're only putting 0% to 5% into the property, which is the best-case scenario of a BRRRR. Investors cannot get the same financing that house hackers can.

## How do I start?

Definitely finish the Ultimate House Hacking Guide for Denver.

Set up a consultation with myself and our team at www.DenverInvestmentRealEstate.com/Consult to answer your questions and create your real estate roadmap.

## Can I house hack if I have student debt?

It depends, but the student debt itself doesn't disqualify you. Joe has given loans to people who have $10k, $50k and $100k in student loan debt. The biggest things to consider are how the debt compares to your income, can you afford payments on your student loans, can you afford payments on a new mortgage and do you have a cosigner. Every situation is different, so talk to a lender.

# Chapter 2

# Financing for House Hackers

In this section, Joe helps us to understand the basics of financing, which loan types are available for house hackers and why house hacking can be so attractive from a financing perspective.

As we've mentioned in the previous chapter, house hacks are purchased as a primary residence and done with an owner-occupant loan. There are great benefits to the owner-occupied loans, and these benefits are some of the main reasons why house hacking is such a popular investing strategy. Joe will go over the differences and advantages of these owner-occupied loans compared to traditional investment loans.

## Owner-Occupied vs. Investment Property Loans

The main differences between owner-occupied and investment property loans are:

- Down payment
- Interest rate
- How long you must occupy the property

For owner-occupied loans, you could put as little as 0%, 3.5%, or 5% down, depending on which loan type you have.

For an investment property loan, you will be required to put 15%, 20%, or 25% down, depending on which loan type you have.

Interest rates for owner-occupied financing are always going to be the lowest rates available. These are the rates you see advertised on TV, the radio and online.

Investment property interest rates will always be a little higher than owner-occupied rates. They typically range between 0.75%-1.5% or higher, depending on the down payment, property type and other various factors.

In summary, you will always have the most favorable rates and least money out of your pocket when you are living in the property, meaning you have used owner-occupied financing. What's the reason for this? Historical data shows that during any major downturn, the rate of foreclosures on owner-occupied homes is far less than those of investment properties. During difficult economic times, people are much more likely to fall behind on an investment property, whereas they will do anything possible to stay current on the mortgage for their home that they live in every day and shelter their family with.

This emotional connection to the property allows banks to take more of a risk on you and offer you a better interest rate, along with lower down payment options and, thus, higher purchasing power.

Another difference between owner-occupied and investment property financing is how long you have to live in the property. Why is there a length of occupancy requirement? The answer is because the lender is giving you a loan with a preferential interest rate and preferential terms based on the risk profile that you will be living in the property.

How long is this requirement? For owner-occupied properties, **it is required that you occupy the home for at least one year**. With any requirement, there will always be some "what-if" questions that come up from people about their specific scenarios. "Well, what if I'm going to buy a house, have my mailing address there, but live with my girlfriend/boyfriend?" Word to the wise, don't mess with fire. You need to live in the property. This is your primary residence, it's where you sleep at night. Don't mess around with legal documents.

Here is a snippet from the loan documents that you'll be signing for an owner-occupant loan:

**6. *Occupancy*** - *Borrower shall occupy, establish and use the Property as Borrower's principal residence within 60 days after the execution of this Security Instrument and shall continue to occupy the Property as Borrower's principal residence for at least one year after the date of occupancy, unless Lender otherwise agrees in writing, which consent shall not be unreasonably withheld, or unless extenuating circumstances exist which are beyond Borrower's control.*

Example of extenuating circumstance: Being relocated for work.

NOT an extenuating circumstance: "I found a really great deal on another property!"

The consequences of violating the occupancy requirements will most likely not affect your current loan, but they will affect your next loan. When your lender goes to approve you for the new loan, they run your name through a database and you will pop up as a red flag because the system will know that it has been less than twelve months since the last loan. Again, don't mess with fire. Buy a house, live there for a year, then you can repeat the process.

# Types of Loans for Owner-Occupants

- **FHA**
  - Minimum 3.5% down
    - Single-Family Residence (SFR), Condo, Townhouse, 2-4 Unit properties
    - Can only have one FHA loan at a time.

Jeff bought his fourplex using FHA, then one year later purchased his next property using a conventional loan as he was not allowed to have more than one FHA loan at a time. Jeff was also really smart using this FHA loan on the fourplex because it allowed him to only pay 3.5% down payment on a higher priced property rather than using the FHA benefits for a single-family home that only has a minimum 5% down payment requirement for a new conventional loan, thus stretching his down payment funds to the largest and best cash-flow property first.

- **Conventional**
  - Minimum 5% down
    - SFR, Condo, Townhouse
  - Minimum 15% down
    - Duplex
  - Minimum 25% down
    - 3-4 Unit properties
- **VA**
  - Minimum 0% down
    - SFR, Condo, Townhouse, 2-4 Unit properties

- Only about 5% of transactions fall under VA loans because only about 5% of the population can qualify for VA loans.

- Need to have served in the military and qualify for VA benefits. If you are eligible, it's a great option.

- **USDA**
  - Minimum 0% down
    - SFR, Townhouse
    - Only rural areas (Denver Metro does not qualify) - underdeveloped, low to moderate income areas
    - Think Elizabeth, Strasburg, Stranton

- **Down Payment Assistance**
  - Minimum $1,000 down
    - SFR, Condo, Townhouse
    - No multi-family as there are certain income restrictions
    - Could increase closing costs and interest rate
    - Not ideal for house hackers due to possibility of a 2nd lien that needs to be paid off when you move out of property

Let's say you get a down payment assistance loan with $10,000 assistance. After 12 months, when you want to move out and buy your next property, you'll need to pay back the $10,000. If you've saved $20,000 for your next down payment, then you'll only have $10,000 left after paying off the lien.

- **Renovation Loans**
  - FHA 203K - Allows up to $35,000 to renovate the property
  - Conventional HomeStyle Renovation - finance up to 50% of property value to renovate the property
    - Tough to make work in the current Denver Metro seller's market. It's easier when it is a buyer's market.
    - Requires you to have all contractor bids in before closing and final loan approval, which can take 15-60 days in Denver; many sellers don't want to wait that long.
    - It's better during a buyer's market.

# Paying Points to Buy Down Your Rate - Does it Make Sense?

If you can understand the financial aspects that go into buying a house, you can use that knowledge to your advantage and make sure you're getting the most return for your money. Another reason why Jeff is so successful is because he has a solid financial background and understands where to look for opportunities to make his money work for him. We will use an example but please note that these numbers are just that, an example to show the concept of how buying down your interest rate can help make an impact, not necessarily that it's a guaranteed outcome.

Disclaimer: Please note that mortgage rates in this example are just that, examples. Actual mortgage rates will fluctuate on a daily basis, depend on your credit score, depend on how much money you are putting down, etc. Contact Joe to get the most recent rates.

A discount point is what you can pay out-of-pocket to lower your interest rate.

| Does NOT Pay to Buy Down Rate | Pays to Buy Down Rate |
|---|---|
| Price: $400,000 | Price: $400,000 |
| Down Payment: 5% | Down Payment: 5% |
| Interest Rate: 3.75% | Interest Rate: 3.125% |
| Discount Points = 0% | Discount Points = 1.50% |
| Cost of Discount Points = $0 | Cost of Discount Points = $5,700 |
| P&I Payment: $1,760 | P&I Payment: $1,672 |
| Saves $133 per month and takes 43 months to break-even | |

Cost of Points = Loan Amount * Discount Point = (380,000 * 0.015) = $5,700.

This cost is paid as an additional closing cost up front to get a lower interest rate (3.75% to 3.125%). You get a lower rate for 30 years for a little more money today, which results in lower monthly payments.

You can then calculate the monthly savings and break-even point of that monthly savings. If your break-even point is less than the amount of time you plan to spend in the property, it's probably a good deal!

If you pay $5,700 up front to save $133 monthly, then $5700/$133 = 42.857 months. If you plan on keeping the property for 43 months or 3.5 years, then it's probably worth it.

If we have $5,700 extra, why not just add that to our down payment and pay down the principal? Ultimately, the $5,700 used to buy down the interest rate will save you more money from a monthly cash-flow perspective. In our example above, you would save about $25-$30 per month to pay down the principal but save $133 per month to buy down the interest rate.

Also, note that there is no cap on how many points you can buy the interest rate down. While there is no cap, there is a point of diminishing returns to where it will no longer make sense to keep buying down the points. At some point, it will no longer make sense to pay hundreds or thousands of dollars to buy down the interest rate to save only $20 per month.

Basically, financing is tricky and the best thing to do is, once you have a property under contract, sit down with your lender so they can go through all these scenarios with you and you can get clarity on which options will be best for your situation.

# Mortgage Insurance - Do I Have to Pay It?

The short answer is yes. You must pay mortgage insurance on any loan when you put less than 20% down, unless it's a VA loan. Anyone who tells you differently isn't necessarily lying, but they may not be disclosing the mortgage insurance to you, so better read the fine print. It could mean you have higher closing costs or a higher interest rate. So, yes you have to pay, but there are three options on how to pay it.

- Lender can pay it for you
- You can pay for it monthly
- You can pay it up front

Disclaimer: Please note that mortgage insurance costs in this example are just that, examples. Actual mortgage insurance costs will fluctuate on a daily basis, depend on your credit score, depend on how much money you are putting down, etc.

| Options to Pay Mortgage Insurance | |
| --- | --- |
| Monthly | Up Front |
| Price: $400,000 | Price: $400,000 |
| Down Payment: 5% | Down Payment: 5% |
| Monthly Insurance Payment: $144 | Up Front Cost: $4,978 |
| **Saves $114 per month and takes 44 months to break-even** | |

The break-even point = (upfront cost * monthly savings) = ($4,978 / $114) = 44 months. If you plan to keep the property for 3 years and 8 months, then it may be worth paying it up front.

Calculating mortgage rates is a complex process that uses 50+ variables to calculate including property zip code, price, property type, number of units, amount of your down payment, credit score, spouse's credit score, income source, income level, type of loan, etc. The only way to know for sure what this will be is to call your lender and have them run the numbers for you **after you're under contract on a property.**

# Can I Combine Buying Down Points and Upfront Mortgage Insurance?

Yes, you can!

Disclaimer: Please note that mortgage rates and mortgage insurance costs in this example are just that, examples. Actual mortgage rates and mortgage insurance costs will fluctuate on a daily basis, depend on your credit score, depend on how much money you are putting down, etc.

| No Points Buy Down and No Upfront Mortgage Insurance Prepayments | Combine Points Buy Down and Upfront Mortgage Insurance Prepayments |
|---|---|
| Price: $400,000 | Price: $400,000 |
| Down Payment: 5% | Down Payment: 5% |
| Interest Rate: 3.75% | Interest Rate: 3.125% |
| Discount Points = 0% | Discount Points = 1.50% |
| Cost of Discount Points = $0 | Cost of Discount Points = $5,700 |
| P&I Payment: $1,760 | Upfront Cost: $4,978 |
| Monthly Insurance Payment: $144 | Additional Cost: $10,678 |
| **Total PMI: $1,874/month** | **Total PMI: $1,627/month** |
| **Saves $247 per month and takes 43 months to break-even** ||

The break-even point for combination of both buying down points and paying mortgage insurance up front will be 3 years and 7 months. If you have an extra $11,000 and plan to own the property for that long, it could be a good option for you. Another option to consider is that the $11,000 does not necessarily have to come from your pocket. There are ways to negotiate these costs into your contract by raising the purchase price or getting some seller concessions. For Jeff's third house hack, we raised the purchase price while under contract by $5,000 and asked the seller for a $5,000 seller credit. He used the credit to prepay mortgage insurance.

There are a lot of levers that can be pulled to change your monthly payment. For these purposes, it's less about understanding the exact numbers and more about grasping the concepts. Once you have wrapped your head around that, you can build your team of experienced agents and lenders, like us, to help you build your rental portfolio. We know what you can and can't do, and how to help you maximize your opportunities.

## Which Option is the Best?

Spending a little more money upfront, can change your monthly payment for the next 30 years.

| Owner-Occ 5% Down | Owner-Occ 5% with Point buydown & Upfront Mtg Ins | Investment Property |
|---|---|---|
| Rate: 3.75% | Rate: 3.125% | Rate: 4.25% |
| Investment: $25,040 | Investment: $35,718 | Investment: $108,000 |
| Payment: $1,874 | Payment: $1,627 | Payment: $1,869 |
| | | |
| Rent: $2,200 | Rent: $2,200 | Rent: $2,200 |
| Cash-Flow: $-147 | Cash-Flow: $121 | Cash-Flow: $273 |
| Total return: 118% | Total return: 94% | Total return: 30% |

Survey says… Option #2 is the best. You are getting a little less from your total return on investment, but overall, it's still a great number at 94%. You have positive cash-flow and lower monthly payments. You need to look at each transaction individually to determine which scenario is best for you and your long-term goals.

# How to Get Started

1. Get pre-approved

   - Pre-qualification is based on verbal information and credit report.

- Pre-approval is based on written information like collecting your actual taxes, W2s, paycheck stubs and your credit report.

- Offers are much stronger with pre-approval letters and, in the Denver market, you won't be a consideration if there is a multiple offer situation without a pre-approval letter.

- The pre-approval letter says to the seller that the buyer has been fully qualified and is ready to go! All they need is a purchase contract, appraisal and title commitment.

2. Having your credit pulled will NOT ruin your life. Your life and credit will not go down the tubes if you have someone pull your credit. If you want to invest, lenders have to be able to see your credit. Lenders have to verify your payment history on previous loans, credit score, outstanding debts, outstanding student loans, etc. If the change of a couple points on your credit score from "pulling your credit score" is the difference in you being approved vs not being approved, you should NOT be investing right now.

   a. As far as credit minimums are concerned, at the time of writing, 620 is the lowest credit score required to be approved for a new loan. To get the very best terms on a loan, a credit score of 740 and above is required.

3. If you want to have a serious conversation about where you stand and how to buy a property, then a lender will need a full application with all of your information, credit report, income, assets, goals, etc.

Overall, making these financial decisions will be the foundation of you starting your house hacking search. Don't set yourself up to be disappointed by not knowing how much you are qualified for. It lets us know where we should look, how much you can afford, and is ultimately the reality check we all need to make sure we help you obtain your investing goals quickly and efficiently.

To get pre-approved, make sure to contact Joe Massey at Castle & Cooke Mortgage.

**Call:** 303-809-7769

**Email:** jmassey@castlecookemortgage.com

# Chapter 3

# The Best Properties for House Hacking

———————◦———————

This chapter discusses the best properties for house hacking in the Denver market today. Several people who come to us have researched house hacking online about the type of property they think they need to be successful with a house hack strategy. While certain properties might be more ideal, the information usually acquired is from talking about house hacking on a national and very general level. Online national information is often like a "square peg in a round hole" situation—it just doesn't work! We want to look at house hacking on the local and specific level and what will work best for our current market in Denver.

One of the misconceptions several people have is that the only good deals to be found are ones that are "off-market" or ones where you need to go around knocking on doors or work with a wholesaler to find them. While these methods work for some investing strategies, we've found that for house hacking, it's not the best or easiest way to find good deals.

# The Deal Quadrant

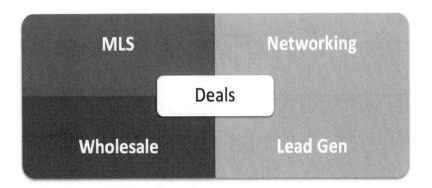

**There are four main ways to find an investment property.**

1. Multiple Listings Service (MLS) - Properties found online through sites like REColorado, which is the Denver MLS.

2. Networking - Properties found through relationships with friends, family, business associates

3. Wholesalers - Properties found through both MLS and "Off-Market" opportunities. Wholesalers spend their time getting property contracts with sellers, then finding investors to buy those contracted properties through an "off-market" format. This person is typically not a real estate agent.

4. Lead Generation - Properties that are found by generating leads yourself. Think of those "we buy ugly houses" or "we pay cash for houses" signs on the side of the road. Usually these are investors trying to find sellers in a distressed situation who need to sell a property fast.

The good news for Denver house hackers is that the most successful way to find good house hack properties is through the MLS. This surprises some clients. They think working with wholesalers or doing some lead generation is where you are going to find the best deal for your money.

The reason working with those two quadrants is very difficult for house hackers is the timeline. Usually Wholesalers and Investors who are able to pay cash for properties are able to make an offer, put "hard" (non-refundable) earnest money down in a couple of hours, and close on property in seven to ten days! For a typical house hacker, who is buying the first or second property, that is simply too fast. As a house hacker, we want to make sure you do all your due diligence, making sure your financing is set up and that you feel comfortable with the transaction.

The good news is that house hackers don't need the same discounts on properties as an investor or flipper because they are already getting the most powerful thing in a real estate transaction, which is a low down payment loan and a 30-year loan. As a house hacker, you are able to get what an investor cannot: a high leverage loan at a low interest rate amortized over 30 years. Many hard money loans for investors are for six to twelve months and have an interest rate greater than 10%.

Let's look at the stats. I pulled our team's stats from February 2019 through February 2020. The top half of this chart is strictly rentals that we helped investors acquire and the bottom half are the house hack numbers. **We helped 20 clients buy house hacks and each one was found on the MLS.** Bringing in another source, when we asked Joe about his house hacking clients, he confirmed that 0 deals were from lead generation, 1 was from a wholesaler and all the rest he's ever done were found on the MLS.

This doesn't mean we weren't looking at these other sources for properties, it's just a fact that 99.9% of the best deals we've found for house hackers in the Denver area have been through the MLS.

# 12-Month Stats

| | MLS | Networking | Wholesaler | Lead Gen |
|---|---|---|---|---|
| Rental | | | | |
| Multi | 2 | 7 | 0 | 0 |
| House | 5 | 0 | 0 | 0 |
| Condo/Townh ome | 12 | 2 | 0 | 0 |
| Rental Subtotal: | 19 | 9 | 0 | 0 |
| | 68% | 32% | 0 | 0 |
| | | | | |
| House Hack/Nomad ™ | | | | |
| Multi | 2 | 0 | 0 | 0 |
| House | 14 | 0 | 0 | 0 |

| Condo/Townh ome | 4 | 0 | 0 | 0 |
|---|---|---|---|---|
| **Subtotal:** | 20 | 0 | 0 | 0 |
| | 100% | 0 | 0 | 0 |
| | | | | |
| **TOTAL:** | 39 | 9 | 0 | 0 |
| | 81% | 19% | 0 | 0 |

Jeff confirmed that all three of his house hacking deals have also come from the MLS. Jeff has experience with creative ways to find properties, including doing some out-of-state investing, wholesales and short sales. Yet, he still focuses on the MLS to find his personal house hacks.

Some of the off-market properties would be a week away from foreclosure and ultimately not even realistic for a traditional investor to obtain. It can become a full-time job where you need to be ready to answer your phone at any given time and negotiate an offer within hours. In fact, it's typically an investor's full-time job, or they have hired a person or team to completely focus on answering the phones and digging into properties.

The properties that Jeff could accept the timeline for through wholesalers were, a lot of times, in such disrepair that they would not qualify for an owner-occupant loan. To qualify for the traditional low down payment financing, the property needs to be habitable and livable.

One example that I have had with one of our clients was we found a property that was basically a "fix and flop." Investors had purchased the property as a high-end flip. They started demolition, but then ran out of money and needed to sell it. Our clients wanted to buy it and live in it while they fixed it up and finished what the previous investor couldn't. The problem was that the property was not habitable. It didn't have kitchen appliances, the water had been turned off due to sewer issues and the gas was turned off as well. All these things meant that the property was uninhabitable and wouldn't qualify for regular financing.

We understood this and they lined up a construction loan to buy the property. After the renovations were completed, they refinanced into a conventional loan. Construction loans often require 30% or more for a down payment and have a higher interest rate. They were experienced and had the cash to take down this property.

So, while the deals are not impossible to find, it really requires someone who can dedicate the time and energy to it, which, like Jeff, a lot of house hackers don't have. They already have full-time jobs. They don't have the ability to take on big renovation projects and spend months sourcing off-market deals. They need an easier way to find livable houses and the MLS provides that.

Let's compare different property types and how they work for house hacking.

# Multi-family

A duplex, triplex or fourplex.

For house hacking specifically, anything that is four units or less is a multi-family property. Once it's five units or more, it no longer qualifies for a residential loan and is a commercial property. Commercial loans offer no favorable owner-occupied financing and typically require a 25% to 30% down payment. The concept of a multiunit makes perfect sense. Buy a multi-family, live in one unit and rent out the others. However, in the current Denver market, multi-family house hacks are tough to find.

**Inventory/Quality: Low**

- Duplexes under $736,000: 19
- Triplexes under $889,000: 7
- Fourplexes under $1,100,000: 11

These price points were picked because these are the limits for each (duplex, triplex, fourplex) to qualify for the FHA loan limits. The numbers above show a snapshot in time of when I pulled the stats. It's a typical representation of multi-family inventory.

**Financing:**

- FHA or VA
- No low down for conventional loans (minimum 15% down for duplex, 25% down for triplex/fourplex)

- You can use FHA on your first property but typically not on your 2nd or 3rd. FHA is not designed to help investors build a rental portfolio.

**Other considerations:**

You need to think about this from the seller's point of view. If there is a multiple offer situation (very common in the Denver market), which offer looks better to a seller: The house hacker with an FHA loan or a traditional investor using a loan with lower health and safety criteria? Sellers will typically go with the offer that will be the least headache and most likely to close. Other things to consider:

- Appraisal standards are much stricter for FHA than conventional on health and safety items.
- You must move in within 60 days. Most multi-family properties have tenants. What is the timing of the leases? You will need to have one tenant move out so you can move in.
- High competition from investors. Investors care a lot less about the property condition than a house hacker who is going to live there.

**10% of our house hack transactions have been multi-family properties over a 12-month period.**

Using the above numbers as an example, if you have a total of 37 (19+7+11) multi-family available, and you consider that they have to pass the more strict health and safety guidelines for FHA, and you consider a unit either needs to be vacant or there is a lease ending within 60 days, how many will be an option? There is no way to pull data, buy my guess based on looking at properties all the time is that at least 50% are not going to be an option. Then, out of those units, you have competition from investors.

We aren't saying these deals don't exist or that you shouldn't do it if the opportunity presents itself, all we want to get across is to not get hyper focused on one type of property. Any property for a year is better than no property because you are waiting on the sidelines for that perfect multi-family. Even if your first house hack is a multi-family, like Jeff's was, all future properties will be single family where you can use a 5% down conventional loan.

# Houses (Detached)

Single family homes, no shared walls, usually in a more suburban neighborhood.

### Inventory/Quality: High

- Houses with 4+ bedrooms, 2+ bathrooms under $400,000: 276
- Price range: low 300s to high 400s
- High 300s to low 400s are most common ($370k-$430k)

I used the 4+ bedroom, 2+ bathroom <$400,000 search filter to show the most common type of homes that we're buying for house hacks. Without the filter, the results would be skewed with all the homes on the market.

### Financing:

- FHA, VA, USDA, Conventional

- Can get 5% down conventional financing on your 1$^{st}$ through 10$^{th}$ properties.

**Other considerations:**

- Usually make the most sense in the current market

**70% of our house hack transactions are detached homes.**

Things may change in five to ten years, but in our current Denver market, these properties typically work the best for house hacking. There's higher inventory, more loan options available, better conditions and are usually not tenant occupied. The odds are much more in your favor.

# Condos and Townhomes (Attached)

Properties that are attached to other units or share at least one common wall with another unit.

### Inventory/Quality: Medium

- For units that are within a price point that make house hacking numbers attractive, usually two types of quality: "renter-grade" and ones that are a little nicer that you could live in for a year or two.
- Typically buy 3 bedroom, 2 bathrooms. These are the "sweet spot" for when you move out and convert it to a rental.
- Price range: Mid 200s to low 300s

## Financing:

- FHA, VA, Conventional
- Some condo complexes are not FHA approved
- Townhomes are treated like single family homes and approved for FHA
- Can get 5% down conventional financing on your 1$^{st}$ through 10$^{th}$ property.
- First-Time Home Buyer programs - 3% down payment
- Down Payment Assistance programs may be available for first property

## Other considerations:

- Keep an eye on HOA fees and HOA health. A monthly HOA of $300-$350 is typically the highest you'll want to go.
- Does HOA allow for rentals? Most in Denver do but sometimes there's a limit of how many properties can be "investor owned". May also not allow Short-term/Airbnb rentals.

### 20% of our house hack transactions

The biggest hurdle when looking to house hack a condo or townhome will be the HOA. On top of making sure that your HOA is approved for FHA financing, and that the monthly amount works for your cash-flow numbers, you also need to consider the impact it can have on your overall monthly payment and ability to qualify for the mortgage.

Using Joe's example, let's say you qualify for a total mortgage payment of $2,000. If you are looking at single family, detached homes, you could afford around a $400,000 house because your mortgage payment will be about $2,000. If you found a property with an HOA of $250, you are now only able to afford a condo/townhome around $350,000. It would have a monthly mortgage of about $1,750 because the HOA of $250 has to be considered for the total payment of $2,000.

You will also need to consider the overall "health" of the HOA. The HOA is essentially a third party to the loan that can impact the value of the home. Lenders now do extensive HOA background checks to make sure that they are keeping up with maintenance, making sure they are collecting and putting money into the reserve account for future maintenance items, confirming the HOA has appropriate insurance, and making sure they are paying their bills. Lenders don't like to see super low HOA fees because it makes them think they aren't doing enough for maintenance. Lenders don't like super high HOA fees either because it's an indicator that some residents are in default of payments and the rest of the residents are having to compensate for that. The good news is that your team of professionals (agent, lender, etc.) will help you through checking the HOA. You do not need to research this on your own before going under contract on the property. After you're under contract, part of the due diligence period allows you to dig into the HOA health. Fortunately, we are often familiar with complexes and know the few to absolutely avoid.

Even though it might seem overwhelming to address all these HOA issues, it should not be a deterrent to not look into these properties. Joe, Jeff, and I will all consider a property, regardless of if it has an HOA or not. Joe and I both own investment properties with HOAs and have had zero issues. We will continue to buy more rentals with HOA's.

# Accessory Dwelling Units (ADUs)

ADUs are usually a one-bedroom, one-bathroom unit that is in the back of a house or above a garage. Commonly called carriage houses, granny flats or mother-in-law suites. These have become very popular recently. However, they sound much better on paper than trying to implement in the house hacking strategy.

There are two ways to think about ADUs: purchasing a house with an existing ADU or buying a property and then building an ADU.

**Purchasing a house with an ADU.**

If you can find a house with an ADU already in place, do it! It has a lot of advantages for increasing rental income. Unfortunately, they are very tough to search for on the MLS and the quality range is huge.

- Inventory - First of all, there aren't too many houses with existing ADUs in the Denver Metro area. The next big challenge is finding the houses that do have ADUs. There isn't a good way to source them. Most agents don't mention them in the MLS listings, so it makes it very hard to search for them.

- Financing - Good news, ADUs have no impact on the financing. This means that whether a house has an ADU or does not have an ADU, lenders treat it the same as a typical single-family, detached house. So, you can qualify for an FHA, Conventional, USDA and VA loan just as you normally would.

- If there is a property with an ADU, usually it sells at a premium because people (a.k.a. Investors and house hackers) know the value of that extra income potential on the property. So, it can drive the purchase price way up.

- Location - They tend to be on the west side of town (west of I-25.)

## Building

Almost on a weekly basis, someone asks me about building ADU's. Here's why building one from scratch usually doesn't make sense.

- Zoning - In 2019, Denver County did pass a rule that will allow more ADUs, which is good news.

- Cost - Average cost to build an ADU range from $150k to $200k. How do you fund that? Most people don't have $200,000 in cash, so they need to use financing.

- Financing - There are no low down options to go build one.

  - Conventional loan - If you buy a $400k house in Denver and then want to pay $150k to put an ADU on the property, Joe can only give you a loan for the $400k, with conventional, 5% down. The other $150k is on you.

  - HELOC - Some can take the equity from their home to fund the ADU, but you must have enough equity in your property to take out money. This isn't an option if you just purchased a place for 5% down.

  - Construction loan - You typically need to put 35% down.

- Time - Typical ADU builds can take about one year to build. It takes a long time to get permits, inspections and sign-offs from the city.

- Appraisal - Once construction of the ADU is completed, it's really hard to get the improvement to be a direct value add to the overall property based on the amount you spent to produce it. If you have a $400k house and spend $200k on an ADU, very rarely will the new appraised value be $600k. The highest adjustment Joe has ever seen for the addition of an ADU is $50k. More commonly, he sees about $30k-$35k positive adjustment on the appraised value. You're essentially building a tiny house, but appraisers typically only value the extra bedroom and bathroom just as if it were in the main house.

Overall, you have to look at the numbers. If you have an extra $200k to build an ADU, instead of spending it on an ADU, why not use that $200k to purchase another rental property or a fourplex?! If one ADU can bring an additional average $1,200-$1,500 in monthly rents, a fourplex will bring in 4 times as much. The stronger cash-flow wins!

So, if you look at how best to allocate your capital, it usually will not be from building an ADU. It will be to take that money and buy a rental property with 20%-25% down, then leveraging up when the time is right. Every time I've sat down with a client and ran them through the numbers, every single one has abandoned the ADU build idea. I expect the build cost to come down eventually, so hopefully this option becomes affordable.

# Tiny Homes – Non-Permanent Fixtures

Are you allowed to park a tiny home in the backyard and use it essentially as an ADU? The answer is: it depends on the municipality. Essentially, tiny homes are just like trailers; they are not permanent fixtures. If your county allows you to park a trailer on your property and allows it to be hooked up to water and sewer, then yes, you can have a tiny home on your property. Make sure you check out all the rules and regulations with your municipality before parking a trailer!

To wrap up, what is the best property for house hackers? Well, if you haven't already guessed, it's our famous answer: It depends!

You really need to do a deep dive on your personal situation and figure out which property would meet your needs best. The best thing you can do is know your wants and needs. Do you have a spouse that you need to consider, are kids involved, how important is the commute to work, will you be able to go from your luxury apartment to a run-down duplex with no covered parking? Jeff makes the best point in that you need to be honest with yourself and identify what you can and cannot deal with.

# Chapter 4

# The Best Locations for House Hacking

———◇———

Since we went over which property types work best for house hacking in the last chapter, it only makes sense that we now explore what areas of the Denver Metro area we find those types of house hack properties.

## Balancing Act: Personal versus Investing

A common theme that you hear us talk about is how house hacking is the balancing act of your personal needs versus investing goals. The reason this topic is so important is because, unlike other investment purchases, you will have to live in this house hack property. You have to determine if the house hacking method is even feasible for you and your family. Then you need to determine if the property that you found will work for your personal situation. Do you feel comfortable in that neighborhood, is the commute to work tolerable, is the house set-up for the desired amount of privacy from other occupants? Many times, the best investment property does not work for your personal needs. You have to find the "balance" of your personal needs vs. your investing needs. It's not going to be worth it to be miserable. You have to know where you are willing to compromise or make sacrifices and where you aren't.

# Investing Criteria

When analyzing house hack properties, there are two ways you need to look at it: Short-term, which is simply while you are living in the property, and long-term, which will be after you have moved out of the property. Most house hackers live in a property for one to two years. So, when thinking in the short-term, the question is: Does this property meet my personal needs for the next couple years? Then, thinking more long-term, you want to make sure that the property also makes sense once you move out and that you are getting the desired returns from the property.

The areas that seem really great in the short-term, like areas around downtown that have lots of restaurants, breweries and shops that are all within a walkable distance and, in turn, seem to increase your "quality of life" are NOT always the best rental properties. The margins are too low, and the numbers just don't make sense when you move out and turn it into a rental property.

### Price-to-Rent Ratio

- Do the numbers make sense while you're living there?
- Do they make sense after you move out?

Buying a $400k house that gets rents of $2,200 per month does NOT mean that an $800k house will get $4,400 in rents per month.

For most house hackers, we are seeing that the price point of a house that makes sense vs. one where the numbers just don't work, are hovering around the mid $400s price point or less. A good example is the Washington Park neighborhood. While most of us hear "Wash Park" and think, *oh, that's a great neighborhood; it must be a good rental area too!* that's usually not the case. The average price point for a single-family house in Wash Park is about a million dollars. Average rents are about $3,700 per month. When you look at that ratio, it's not nearly as favorable as a single-family house in north Aurora with a price point in the low $300s and rents of $1,900 per month.

Jeff makes another great point that, in his searching for house hack properties, he has found that there is a large premium for the "popular" neighborhoods, and while we all know that is true for all real estate (location, location, location), it's not the aspect you want to be paying a premium for when looking for a house hack property.

The great thing about Denver, Jeff points out, is that just outside those "popular" neighborhoods, are some really great opportunities where you won't have to pay the premium prices. In Jeff's experience, especially for the room by room level, people will pay about the same in rent to live downtown by a brewery as they would in Jeff's house hack in southwest Denver that is 15 minutes outside of downtown and 10 minutes to a light rail station.

## The Trend is Your Friend

- Think long-term
- What's going on in the neighborhood(s) around you?

Unlike the stock market, which can change minute to minute, real estate changes are relatively slow. This works in our favor because it makes it easier for us to predict these real estate trends:

- When you walk outside, what do you see?
- Is there one lot, four houses down that has been completely scraped and is preparing for something new to be built?

- Are there dumpsters in the block next to yours where they are doing rehab projects?
- Was a four-unit row house just completed at the end of the block?

These are all signs that a neighborhood is in transition and an opportunity to capitalize on the upward trend.

Looking for these neighborhoods with these upward trends and transformations can be excellent areas for good house hacks. A lot of times it's areas that are right outside the really expensive neighborhoods. A good example of this is the River North (RiNo) area. Years ago, Downtown Denver was just too expensive, so what happened? People started to invest and develop more north into Five Points and what is now known as the extremely popular and "trendy" RiNo neighborhood.

Jeff's most recent house hack is in another great area of southwest Denver. It's more suburban but is one of the last pockets of affordable properties that is close to downtown, light rails and other popular neighborhoods like Bel Mar.

The concept is that transitioning neighborhoods usually mean good appreciation, higher purchase points and higher rents for the long-term.

### Government Programs

The government will often spend money or reduce investors' taxes to invest money to develop certain areas. These are areas and programs that we don't limit our searches to, but if there is an opportunity in one of these areas, it can add some great long-term benefits.

Opportunity zones are areas that are underdeveloped and have been identified as an area where they would like to see money funneled into to help with development. Not that you would necessarily take advantage of the tax advantages from directly investing in the opportunity zones, but you can capitalize on what that means for the area.

There are usually great tax advantages to people and organizations that invest in opportunity zones. If people invest in an area, it will usually change for the better and you as a house hacker can ride the coattails of those positive changes from the "big money."

Another aspect to watch for is what each municipality is doing. Lakewood is a good example. In 2019, they passed Proposition 200, which now limits development in Lakewood. If the city limits supply of housing but there is still high demand to live in Lakewood, that should increase rents and house prices in that area.

Lakewood is located between Denver and Golden, which are two highly desirable places to live and the average price points for houses are greater than Lakewood. Lakewood is still a great location with easy access to downtown and to the mountains. If Proposition 200 limits the available homes in this area, there's a good chance that Lakewood home prices will increase significantly, and it may see above average appreciation.

One other government program is the Colfax Avenue Business Improvement District that is helping to develop businesses and areas along Colfax Ave. Ultimately, more money invested into these areas will hopefully create an upward trend and transition these areas for the better.

Again, while these factors should not be a make or break when determining if the property is a good fit for your situation, having properties in your portfolio that take advantage of these types of programs or are in these areas will only be another added benefit in the long run.

## Closed House Hack Map

Below is a screenshot of Google Maps where I inputted the majority of house hacks closed over the last two years.

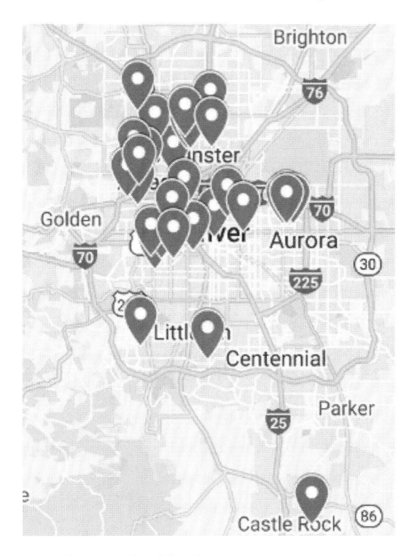

House hacks we've closed for clients.

**Here's the same map zoomed in:**

You can see that the vast majority of these properties are located on the north side of town. Most have been closer to the mountains and west of I-25 in Lakewood, Arvada, Wheat Ridge, Westminster, Thornton and Northglenn. We've also done a large number in North Aurora near the Anschutz Medical Complex close to Colfax and I-225. The North Aurora area is a great example of what we just discussed previously. It's in a transitioning area, located near a major economic driver (the Anschutz Medical Complex) and many parts of it are in Opportunity Zones.

It's interesting to compare the locations of house hacks in relation to the locations for traditional rentals.

## Map of House Hack Locations

## Map of Rental Property Locations

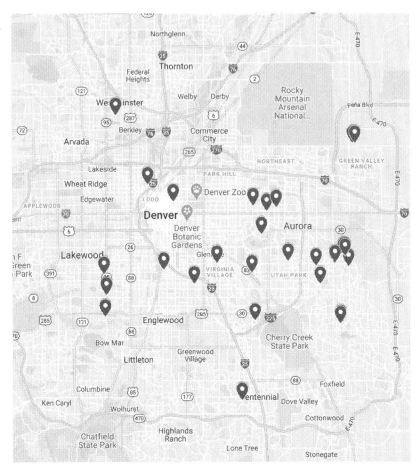

Interestingly, it's almost a mirror image or opposite of what we see for house hacks. Most of the good rentals we see are on the East side of Denver Metro. This proves our point from the beginning of this chapter that, from a purely rental number standpoint, traditional rentals will be better rentals than a good house hack. So, why don't house hackers buy these rental properties and use them as house hacks? Well, it's because most of these rental properties will not fit for the personal needs of a house hacker.

# What's the Best Location?

If you can't guess this answer, you haven't been paying attention to the previous chapters. It has to be our classic answer: It depends!

You need to determine your tolerances, your preferences, your work commute, the aspects that affect your quality of life, and how the location of the house hack fits into the balance of your personal and investment goals and strategies. There's no right or wrong answer. The other interesting thing, which Jeff points out, is that your goals and tolerances may change. What you are willing to sacrifice or deal with on your first house hack, might be different by house hack number two or three. You have to continuously evaluate your goals and adjust accordingly.

# Chapter 5

# Maximizing Rents

There are two scenarios that we need to consider when we are evaluating how to maximize rents for house hacking.

The first scenario is, of course, while you are living in the property. Lending guidelines require that you move into the property within 60 days of closing the transaction, and then you are required to stay in that property as your primary residence for at least 365 days.

The second scenario is after you have moved out of the property. This scenario is ultimately the more important of the two because you will only be living in the property for a relatively short period of time. You need to make sure the numbers work on a long-term basis.

There are several strategies for collecting rents for each scenario, and we will talk specifically about renting room by room, short-term rentals, medium-term rentals and long-term rentals.

## Renting Room by Room

This strategy works best with a single-family home with several rooms and bathrooms. In the current Denver market, we are seeing the room by room model as the most popular for hitting a "sweet spot" and maximizing the room-to rent-ratio. Our expert House Hacking

Coach, Jeff White, uses this strategy in his second house hack property after moving out and his third house hack property while living there.

A few reasons room by room rentals work so well are because of the demographics and the price points. Jeff has found that the demographics of the room by room tenants tend to be young professionals between 25-35 years of age. These tenants are only required to pay between $700-$850 per month in rent whereas, if they were to get a one-bedroom apartment on their own, they would be paying between $1,200-$1,600 per month to live in the Denver Metro area.

**Typical rents** - We usually see between $700-$850 per month in rents and that is pretty consistent around the Denver area. In general, for a 10'x12' bedroom with a shared bathroom, we will see between $700-$750 per month. For a master bedroom with a private bathroom, we are seeing about $850 per month. Rooms with private bathrooms command the most rent.

Facebook Marketplace is a great resource for rental comps and shows how you should structure your listing and has great visuals. Craigslist is good for comparing rental comps and is nice because it has a map feature, which allows you to get a decent perspective on what different areas are getting for room rentals.

In our experience, we have found that location doesn't have as much impact on room rental versus an entire unit rental.

## What is a Bathroom Worth in a Denver House Hack?

In December 2018, one of my clients, Austin Allan, asked at a house hacking class, "How much impact do private bathrooms have on rent when renting it out room by room?"

My response, "I have no idea! Sounds like a great thing for you to research and tell me." To my surprise and delight, he did!

Below is an analysis by Austin Allan on how much a bathroom is worth when it comes to renting out room by room.

######### Start Austin's Analysis #########

After talking a little bit at the end of the house hacking class you gave this last week, I began to really think about what a bathroom is worth when renting a room out. I am trying to put together the best plan I can so that, when I am able to purchase that first property, I have it optimized as far as rents and location goes.

I decided to do a little project to see if I could figure out what a bathroom is worth here in the Denver market. I analyzed 50 room-for-rent posts on Craigslist and ran a linear regression to see how a private bathroom affected the cost of a room rental. This is by no means the most comprehensive analysis that could be done, but it does provide at least some insight and can help with future decision making.

The factors that I used for collection data were:

- Cost of the room
- Private bathroom
- Laundry in the unit
- Distance from downtown
- Access to the light rail.

There are notes in the spreadsheet that go into more detail on each of the variables. Given the inconsistent nature of Craigslist posts, many had to be excluded because of incomplete information.

After running the regression, several interesting things stood out to me.

1. **Laundry and light rail access are worth very little when it comes to the value of a room.** They both had a negative value, only indicating that there was no consistency in the pricing of rooms which had those features. Neither of those would ever decrease the price of the room, so the variable is not very helpful in determining the value of a room.

2. **The change in price as you move further away from downtown is much smaller than I expected it to be.** I think that there are a couple of explanations for this; Denver is not a very large metropolitan area, so, even when you live in an outer suburb of the city, you are still less than 20 miles from the downtown area. When compared to larger metropolitan areas such as LA, New York, or Houston, the sprawl is much larger, and people commute from much greater distances. I also believe that the majority of people commute to work via car and not public transportation, so a drive of less than 20 minutes should take around 30 minutes or so with a consideration for some light traffic. I believe that, for most people, this is an acceptable commute time, so the cities that are outside of the downtown area still remain a desirable and reasonable place to live, even when working downtown.

3. **The more important takeaways from the data are that bathrooms appear to be worth between $100-$150, with consideration to the standard deviation.** With more rental data, I could surely get to a more accurate number, but I think, considering the fairly small sample size, this

number seems pretty close to me. The intercept also indicates that, as long as you have a room to rent, you should be able to get at least $700 a month for it, no matter where it is or what you have to offer.

There are many factors that I could not account for that could change the price of the room:

- The age of the home I believe could be a pretty big factor when determining the value of a room. A new build should be able to charge a premium vs. a house that is 100 years old. However, the older homes tend to be in neighborhoods that are closer to downtown, so it's not so easy to tease that information to determine exactly what kind of impact age has.

- The size of the room being offered should have an effect on the price as well. Several of the posts had masters for rent, which had the bathroom, and these are worth more than a room with an unattached bathroom. Square footage of an individual room is hardly ever listed, so trying to determine the true value of a larger room would be hard to do.

- Some neighborhoods are more desirable to live in, so they do command a premium, even while offering only basic accommodations.

All in all, I think this does help reinforce some of the decisions that are made in consideration to where to purchase, how big of a property and how much one can charge for individual rooms. I think that there is a lot more research that could be done to learn more insights into the market of individual room rent. I would love to hear your thoughts on the findings and what else you think could be interesting to look further into.

--------- **End Austin's Analysis** ---------

Thanks, Austin! He did a great job with his analysis. If you want a copy of the spreadsheet, send me an email.

**Utilities** - In most cases, the landlord will pay these bills and charge a monthly amount on top of rent. Landlords usually add up all the utilities for one year and divide by 12 months to get a monthly average to add to rent. Some months will be more expensive, some will be less expensive, so the average will even everything out at the end of the year.

This is also the easiest way to charge for utilities because you don't have to collect the bills, divide them up, send separate invoices to your tenants, then hunt down payment for $30-$50 each month. It can also eliminate issues if a tenant takes a three-week vacation to Europe and doesn't want to pay for utilities they didn't use. We recommend following the keep it simple stupid (KISS) principle with utilities.

One utility to remember is house Wi-Fi. It's not practical to have four different people with four different routers in the same house. Most of us would consider Wi-Fi a necessity these days, so it's best to include it as an added benefit to your tenants.

**Considerations** - Make sure you check your specific municipality for the occupancy limits. You need to verify how many "unrelated parties" can live together. The average is usually three to five parties, but laws change, so make sure to double check. Denver County, for example, is currently in discussion to raise the limit of unrelated parties from two to eight people. You need to be aware of the rules and the consequences.

As far as managing your rental, you need to consider how you will manage the property once you move out. Most property managers do not take on room by room rentals, which means you will have to self-manage; that can be time-intensive, so be prepared.

When thinking about furnishing the property, it's usually a good idea to do, but keep things simple. If you furnish the property, it limits how much a tenant has to bring in and is easier when they have to move out as they don't have as much stuff. It can also help minimize conflicts between tenants if something gets damaged.

Setting good expectations and good examples from the beginning is arguably one of the most important parts of living with others. You need to have these in place from the first conversation you have with your potential tenants. Set house rules and lead by example. Tenants will more than likely follow your lead. If you clean up after yourself, so will they.

You always want to be thinking about the long-term. This includes keeping your next house hack in mind. To make sure that you are getting the most out of your current house hack and setting yourself up for success on the next one, it's important that you track everything you do and all the money you collect. You need to have written leases and proof of deposited security checks. You also need to claim this extra income on your taxes. If you don't keep accurate records of these items, you won't be able to use this rental income towards your debt-to-income ratio when qualifying for your next property.

Overall, the room by room rental model can be more management intensive as you are doing all the work, but it has a good reward in the extra rental income you can achieve. An average four-bedroom, two bathroom single-family house will get around $2,200-$2,600 per month for a long-term tenant. Renting that same house out room by room, you can get $2,800 - $3,200 per month.

## House with a Mother-in-Law Suite

There are certain areas in the Denver Metro area that have more of these layouts with a mother-in-law suite, which can be a huge advantage to your house hacking strategy. The nice thing about these properties is that they have separate entrances, kitchens and bathrooms, so you can really live uninterrupted from your tenants. However, there are some downsides as well.

**Typical Rents** - The rents for these units are in line with other properties that have a similar bedroom and bathroom mix.

**Utilities** - Since these homes are single-family homes, there is typically only one electric, gas and water meter. The easiest solution is to include the utilities in the rent, just as we discussed in the room by room section above.

**Considerations** - It's important to understand that the vast majority of these mother-in-law suites are not permitted.

Houses with mother-in-law suites can provide significant cash-flow but have their cons too. If you want more details, please reach out to us.

## Short-Term Rentals - Airbnb

This method is for any rental period of 30 days or less. It's hard to give a typical rent range on this method because it's highly dependent on location, and rental rates are very dynamic. These rentals demand higher rates for the convenience, but they also require more operating expenses and time management. Many of our house hacking clients do not choose this model for two main reasons:

1. The extra income they earn per month ends up not being worth the time required to manage the rental, or, as I say, "The juice isn't worth the squeeze!"

2. The areas that demand the highest short-term rental rates are in downtown Denver and other hot spots, which is not where our typical house hack properties are found because they are typically more expensive and have poor long-term price-to-rent ratios.

**Typical rents** - Are highly dependent on location and can change neighborhood to neighborhood. A great resource is AirDNA.co which pulls all the data from short-term rentals in a certain zip code to compare rental comps. It costs around $200/mo. to access all of Denver Metro. Fortunately, we have a subscription and are happy to run rental comps for our clients. Please reach out if you need any.

Short-term rentals also have higher operating costs that you want to keep in mind when underwriting the property. There are host website fees from Airbnb/VRBO. There are cleaning fees for each turnover of tenants. There will also be higher maintenance costs as there is more traffic and higher likelihood of "wear and tear." You will be expected to supply all necessities such as toilet paper, soap, shampoo, dishes, pots, pans, silverware and linens. If any of these things run out, break or get taken, you will have to replace them. These expenses can add up quickly.

Basically, you will function like a mini hotel. This means that, on top of all the amenities, you need amazing pictures and should highlight those extra special things you do for your guests such as providing snacks, shampoo, a welcome book, etc. Remember, you're running a hospitality business.

**Utilities** - You as the landlord will pay everything and include the costs in the rental rate. You'll also want to remember to include the Wi-Fi costs as it will be expected from guests to be included with their stay.

**Considerations** - One of the most important things to remember is getting familiar with the rules! Both for the HOA and for your specific municipality. Don't commit fraud, know the rules, play by the rules. For example, in Denver County, the property that you are using to short-term rent must also be your primary residence. If you own a multi-family in Denver, you cannot live in one unit and Airbnb the other unit; it's against the rules! You're only able to Airbnb the unit in which you live. Rules are continuing to change, and municipalities are cracking down on enforcement, so make sure you stay up-to-date.

It's also important to have a "Plan B." You want to make sure the numbers work as a long-term rental in case you are not able to do short-term rental.

Remember that you are running a hospitality business. You're not just a landlord. You will be expected to be available at all times to give instructions for check in/out, give directions, coordinate with the cleaning company on "turns," etc. You will want to consider the possibility of using a management company to help with this, which is another expense.

Finally, you will need to have the place furnished not only with beds, couches, tables and chairs, but also with dishes, pots, pans, silverware, towels and toiletries. Just keep these extra expenses in mind when running your numbers.

# Medium-Term Rentals

Medium-term rentals are fully furnished units and have tenants who stay for 1-6 months.

A popular example is traveling nurses who will typically rent for around 3 months. Another example is corporate housing for people who are being relocated or are staying to work on a project for a few months at a time.

**Typical rents** – Are, again, very dependent on location. For example, traveling nurses want to be close to the hospital they will work at. A businessman will want to be in the city with a short commute, not the suburbs. A great resource for these types of properties to compare rents is FurnishedFinder.com https://www.furnishedfinder.com/ .

In general, we see higher rents than long-term rentals and lower rents than Airbnb, or short-term rentals.

**Utilities** - All will be paid by the landlord and included with the rental rate. Wi-Fi will be expected to be included as well.

**Considerations** - Again, you will need to be an expert on the rules and regulations of both your municipality and your HOA. Many short-term rentals had to pivot to medium-term rentals when Denver changed their rules and required that short-term rentals be your primary residence.

You will want to determine if you are up for self-management or if you want to hire a property management to help you find and turn tenants. In some cases, it can be easier to fill your unit if you work with a property management company or real estate company as they already have relationships built with companies who do corporate relocation.

A typical stay/lease for a medium-term rental is 2-3 months. You will want to make sure the place is fully furnished and ready to use as tenants will expect a "move-in-ready" property.

While we do have a few clients who have rented primarily to nurses based on the location of the property, we do not see many of our clients choose this method for house hacking simply because the margins become very tight. A few years ago, Joe setup one of his units as a medium rental. Guess what? He no longer does it. All the expenses and headache were not worth the extra income. Again, "The juice wasn't worth the squeeze."

# Long-Term Rentals

Long-term is defined as six months or more typically. These are the standard rentals that we commonly talk about with one tenant on one lease for one year.

**Typical rents** for the not super trendy areas but standard properties in areas highlighted on the house hacking map can expect these rents:

- 2 bedrooms: $1,300 to $1600 (typically condos)
- 3 bedrooms: $1,750 to $2,000 (combination of condos and houses)
- 4 bedrooms: $2,200 to $2,600 (houses)
- 5 bedrooms: $2,500 to $2,700 (houses)

Zillow.com is great for rent estimates. Do not use the Zestimate feature for property price. However, their rental estimate is usually accurate within +/- $100. Their rental estimates often get wonky for multi-family properties though. Once you are under contract on a property, a good idea is to contact a property manager to see what rents they are seeing in that particular area. This is something that we help our clients with once we're under contract.

**Utilities** - Can be billed in several different ways but, typically, the tenant pays or reimburses the landlord for water and sewer. The tenant usually puts the electric/gas bill and trash in their name and pays directly. If snow removal and lawn maintenance are not included in the HOA/rental rate, tenants are typically expected to be responsible for these items as well.

**Considerations** – Long-term rentals are the most common in the current Denver market. When you are thinking about purchasing a property, look at the numbers from a long-term perspective, even if you choose to rent room by room. The reason for this is that many people are able to rent room by room initially but get fatigued from it and want to pivot to a property manager or a strategy that is less time-intensive. As we mentioned before, most property managers will not take on properties to rent room by room, so you need to feel comfortable with the long-term method for your long-term goals.

Jeff makes a good point that, during the accumulation phase of your investing, the higher rents can be important, but once you get to the point where you want to be less involved in the day-to-day management of tenants, you will hopefully have acquired enough properties that the small decrease in cash-flow won't make a big impact in the long-term.

So, to wrap up, which method is the best?

You should already know what's coming. It depends.

You have to decide what strategy will fit with your available time, cash-flow goals, risk tolerance and mental sanity! There will be a different scenario for every location. We sit down with our clients to run the numbers as well as double check those numbers with industry professionals, so our numbers are very dialed in. Working with our team and network, you can be confident that you're underwriting the property conservatively and accurately.

# Chapter 6

# Deal Analysis

When you're house hacking, there are two ways to analyze a property:

1. While you're living there.
2. After you move out and convert it to a rental property.

All of us agree that the focus for deal analysis should be on #2 - after you move out and convert it to a rental property. Remember, you are buying a future rental, so the numbers need to make sense as a rental. It's common for new house hackers to get tunnel vision and only focus on the analysis while living there. Don't! The real wealth-building comes from buying multiple house hacks that make sense as rental properties.

## Property Analysis Spreadsheet

The spreadsheet we use is Joe's rental property analysis spreadsheet. It's a great spreadsheet that allows us to put in all appropriate numbers to analyze a property but is simple enough that it doesn't take an analyst to fill out. It has pull down menus for multiple lending scenarios (buying as primary residence vs. investment property) and is somewhat "dummy-proof" in that, if you put in a number that doesn't make sense, it will pop up with a warning. An example is if you enter a 5% down payment but have chosen "investment property", you will get a notification that you need to put at least 15% down.

We also offer the house hacking spreadsheet. The house hacking spreadsheet is designed for longer-term financial modeling of buying four house hack properties. Chapter 8, Long Term Financial Modeling, will go into detail on using that spreadsheet.

As you start analyzing properties, use Joe's spreadsheet for analyzing individual properties. The screenshots in this chapter are from Joe's rental property analysis spreadsheet. This chapter is not meant to be a tutorial on how to use the spreadsheet. You can download the spreadsheet for free and watch YouTube tutorials at www.DenverInvestmentRealEstate.com/RentalSpreadsheet

# Assumptions: Garbage In = Garbage Out.

Your analysis is only as good as the assumptions that you use. Our recommendation is to use realistic and conservative assumptions in your deal analysis. Below is a table with general assumption ranges that are common in the Denver market as of 2020. The table is provided as a quick reference so you're not using inaccurate rules from nationwide websites. **Understand that these are estimated ranges. Always check with us or your real estate team.**

| Spreadsheet Field Name | Amount | Notes |
|---|---|---|
| **Acquisition Costs**<br><br>Condo / Townhome<br>Detached House<br>Multi-family | <br><br>$3,000<br>$4,000<br>$5,500 | Includes inspection, appraisal, closing costs, title fees, etc.<br>IR buy down & prepay PMI will increase acquisition costs. |
| **Vacancy** | 5% | This is a conservative number. For the last few years, many landlords have been less than 3%! |
| **Property Management** | 10% | Most PMs charge 7%-8% but round up to 10% to handle misc. costs. |
| **Repairs / Reserves**<br><br>Condo / Townhome<br>Detached House<br>Multi-family | <br><br>5%<br>8%-10%<br>8%-10% | The HOA handles exterior items for condos and townhomes, thus reducing your repairs reserves.<br>10% is used if property is older and/or has more deferred maintenance items. |
| **Taxes** | | Get from MLS or public records. Make sure it's the most recent year. |
| **Insurance**<br><br>Condo / Townhome<br>Detached House<br>Multi-family | <br><br>$300 - $500<br>$1500 - $2,000<br>$1500 - $2,000 | |

| Utilities | | Utilities will vary from property to property. These are estimates for while living there. Trash is included in the City of Denver's property taxes. |
| --- | --- | --- |
| Water / Sewer | $600 - $1200 | |
| Trash | $300 | |
| Electric / Gas | $1,500 | |

# Deal Analysis: Room by Room House Hack in Aurora

Our client, Austin, purchased this house hack in Q1 of 2020. It's a 5-bedroom, 2-bathroom house in North Aurora. It's close to the Anschutz Medical Campus near Colfax Ave and I-225. This part of town has some of the lower price points around the metro area and high room by room rental demand because of the hospitals. It's a great house hack and long-term rental. The layout is great for renting room by room. The house is in good condition and required no major work when he moved in.

Austin purchased the house for $375,000 with a 5% down conventional loan. After he was under contract, he reviewed all of his lending options with Joe and decided to pay his mortgage insurance monthly, rather than upfront at closing. His actual mortgage insurance came in lower than the estimated amount in Joe's spreadsheet that is shown below, which means even more cash-flow!

Austin currently lives in one bedroom and rents out three other bedrooms at $800 per room, which includes utilities. Four people can live comfortably at the house. Once they are all settled, he'll test renting out the additional bedroom for around $700/mo. or so. Once he moves out, the plan is to continue to rent it room by room to maximize cash-flow.

Let's review the spreadsheet....

| Property Address | Room By Room HH Aurora |
| --- | --- |
| Number of Units | 1 |
| Initial Occupancy Status | Primary Residence |
| | |
| Down Payment Percentage | 5% |
| | |
| Type of Mortgage Insurance | Monthly Paid |
| | |
| Purchase Price | $ 375,000 |
| Acquisition Costs | $ 7,475 |
| Loan Costs | $ 1,540 |
| Down Payment | $ 18,750 |
| Mortgage Balance | $ 356,250 |
| Seller Credits | $ 1,000 |
| Initial Repair Costs | |
| Total Initial Investment | $ 26,765 |
| | |
| Mortgage Interest Rate | 3.875% |
| Mortgage Term (years) | 30 |

The acquisition costs of $7,475 are higher than the estimated ones of $4,000 because Austin chose to buy his interest rate down.

**MONTHLY Rental Income Per Unit AFTER you move out**

| | | |
|---|---|---|
| Unit #1 | $ | 3,200 |
| Unit #2 | $ | - |
| Unit #3 | $ | - |
| Unit #4 | $ | - |
| **Total Rental Income** | $ | 3,200 |

| | |
|---|---|
| **Vacancy Factor** | 5% |
| **Annual Rent Increase** | 3% |
| **Annual Appreciation Rate** | 5% |
| **Effective Tax Rate** | 25% |

The monthly rent is $800 x four bedrooms. Austin may bring in additional income from the fifth bedroom, but it's best to use conservative numbers. If the fifth bedroom works as a rental, great! If not, his property still cash-flows and meets his return expectations.

## Monthly Operating Expenses

| | |
|---|---|
| Do you pay for property management? | No |
| Monthly Reserves for Maintenance - Percentage | 8.0% |
| Is there an HOA | No |

## Additional Annual Expenses

| | | |
|---|---|---|
| Annual Real Estate Taxes | $ | 2,224 |
| Annual Property Insurance | $ | 978 |
| Utilities (If paid by owner) | | |
| - Water and Sewer | $ | 1,200.00 |
| - Trash | $ | 300.00 |
| - Electric | $ | 1,500.00 |
| Landscaping | $ | - |
| Internet | $ | 600.00 |
| Other | $ | - |

Austin's insurance premium is one of the lowest I've ever seen for a home here in Denver. The house had a newer roof (age of roof and material are a big premium driver due to hailstorms), and he shopped around to find a low rate.

| Net Operating Income | $ | 26,606 | | | | | | |
|---|---|---|---|---|---|---|---|---|
| Less: Annual Mortgage Payments | $ | (20,103) | | $356,250 | @ | 3.875% | = $1,675.22 | per month |
| Less: Annual Mortgage Payments | $ | (1,532) | | Estimated Mortgage Insurance | | = | $128 | per month |
| **Annual Cash Flow Before Taxes** | $ | **4,971** | | | | | | |

| | | *1st Year Returns* | | | | | |
|---|---|---|---|---|---|---|---|
| **Cash-on-Cash Rate of Return** | 18.6% | | $4,971 | + | $26,765 | = | 19% |
| **CAP Rate** | 7.1% | | $26,606 | ÷ | $375,000 | = | 7.1% |
| **GRM - Gross Rent Multiplier** | 117.2 | | $375,000 | ÷ | $3,200 | = | 117.2 |

**1st Year Return On Investment Quadrant™ (ROIQ)**

| Appreciation 70.1% | Cash Flow 18.6% | | Appreciation $18,750 | Cash Flow $4,971 |
|---|---|---|---|---|
| | **123.4%** | | | **$33,030** |
| Debt Paydown 24.0% | Depreciation 10.8% | | Debt Paydown $6,411 | Depreciation $2,898 |

**Return On Investment Quadrant™ is a trademark of Real Estate Financial Planner LLC

The estimated cash-flow of $4,971 is for AFTER he moves out of the house. To calculate his return while living there, we just need to reduce the rental income from $3,200 to $2,400/mo. to account for the bedroom that he's living in. The reduced rental income brings the cash-flow to -$3,381 per year. He's living for less than $300/mo! You can't find a room that cheap to rent around town.

Overall, this is a great house hack, and it demonstrates why buying a four- or five-bedroom house and renting it room by room is often one of the best strategies in the current market.

This deal analysis is discussed in great detail on episode #144: "Deal Analysis - Room by Room House Hack in Aurora" on the Denver Real Estate Investing Podcast.

Also, make sure you read Austin's chapter on his house later in this book. To learn more or to connect with Austin Allan, contact him at austin.allen87@gmail.com.

# Deal Analysis: Arvada Airbnb House Hack

Our clients, Ben and Allyson, purchased this house hack in Q2 of 2019. We're using this as an example to share historical operating data for running their Airbnb rental. Ben and Alyson moved to Denver a couple years ago and know the power of house hacking. Their main goal was to reduce their living expenses to less than $1,000/mo. and to start building a rental portfolio.

They purchased a house with a mother-in-law suite. The main house has three bedrooms and two bathrooms. The mother-in-law suite has one bedroom and one bathroom. It's a perfect layout for house hacking. The mother-in-law suite is above the garage with a separate entrance and private path along the side of the house.

The main house was in great shape and had recent updates from the seller. It was turn-key and move-in-ready. The mother-in-law suite was functional and livable, but outdated. To maximize their Airbnb income and long-term rental income, they decided to renovate the mother-in-law suite. They did all the work themselves and spent around $5,000 on materials.

The house was listed at $424,900, but there were multiple offers. Ben and Alyson ended up buying the house for $435,000. Don't let bidding wars or multiple offers scare you away from a property. In the current market, low-ball offers do not work. It's in a great location in Arvada. It's near Ralston Park, and you can easily bike to Olde Town Arvada. Location, Location, Location!

This house works out well for while they are living there and as a rental after moving out. Let's analyze the property while they are living there and once they move out.

Analysis: While Living There

| Property Address | Arvada AirBnB |
|---|---|
| Number of Units | 2 |
| Initial Occupancy Status | Primary Residence |
| | |
| Down Payment Percentage | 5% |
| | |
| Type of Mortgage Insurance | Monthly Paid |
| | |
| Purchase Price | $ 435,000 |
| Acquisition Costs | $ 5,697 |
| Loan Costs | $ 1,540 |
| Down Payment | $ 21,750 |
| Mortgage Balance | $ 413,250 |
| Seller Credits | $ 2,000 |
| Initial Repair Costs | $ 5,000 |
| Total Initial Investment | $ 31,987 |
| | |
| Mortgage Interest Rate | 4.500% |
| Mortgage Term (years) | 30 |

Their acquisition costs are higher than our estimates from earlier because they decided to buy their interest rate down. They received $2,000 in seller credits for minor inspection items. The seller credit reduced the cash they needed by close to $2,000. The initial repairs were about $5,000. Including the initial repair cost is a good idea because you need to spend the money to get the projected rent.

| | | |
|---|---|---|
| Unit #1 | $ | 1,950 |
| Unit #2 | $ | 700 |
| Unit #3 | $ | - |
| Unit #4 | $ | - |
| **Total Rental Income** | $ | 2,650 |
| **Vacancy Factor** | | 3% |
| **Annual Rent Increase** | | 3% |
| **Annual Appreciation Rate** | | 5% |
| **Effective Tax Rate** | | 25% |

The unit #1 rent field shows the Airbnb income after fees and taxes. On average, they were making about $1,950/mo. They really enjoy the Airbnb hosting experience and making new friends. One of the guests that stayed with them on business ended up hiring Alyson's sister for a new business!

The unit #2 rent field shows the rental income from charging Alyson's sister rent for one of the rooms. It's below market rent for a room rental, but it's family and it's a win-win situation. They could have rented out the additional bedroom more cash-flow but didn't want to. The extra income wasn't worth the inconvenience of having a roommate they didn't know. Remember, it's a balancing act!

## Monthly Operating Expenses

| | |
|---|---|
| **Do you pay for property management?** | No |
| **Monthly Reserves for Maintenance - Percentage** | 8.0% |
| **Is there an HOA** | No |

## Additional Annual Expenses

| | | |
|---|---|---|
| **Annual Real Estate Taxes** | $ | 1,455 |
| **Annual Property Insurance** | $ | 1,440 |
| **Utilities (If paid by owner)** | | |
| - Water and Sewer | $ | 672.00 |
| - Trash | $ | 281.00 |
| - Electric | $ | 1,500.00 |
| Landscaping | $ | - |
| Other | $ | - |
| Other | $ | - |

Their water bill is on the lower side because they did not water the lawn for the entire year. Going forward, they'll be watering it regularly. They expect the water bill to be about double.

| | | | | | | | |
|---|---|---|---|---|---|---|---|
| Total Annual Expenses | $ | 7,892 | | | | | |
| Net Operating Income | $ | 22,954 | | | | | |
| Less: Annual Mortgage Payments | $ | (25,127) | $413,250 | @ | 4.500% | = | $2,093.88 per month |
| Less: Annual Mortgage Payments | $ | (1,777) | Estimated Mortgage Insurance | | = | | $148 per month |
| Annual Cash Flow Before Taxes | $ | (3,949) | | | | | |

**1st Year Returns**

| | | | | | | |
|---|---|---|---|---|---|---|
| Cash-on-Cash Rate of Return | -12.3% | -$3,949 | + | $31,987 | = | -12% |
| CAP Rate | 5.2% | $22,954 | ÷ | $440,000 | = | 5.2% |
| GRM - Gross Rent Multiplier | 166.0 | $440,000 | ÷ | $2,650 | = | 166.0 |

1st Year Return On Investment Quadrant™ (ROIQ)

| Appreciation 68.0% | Cash Flow -12.3% | | Appreciation $21,750 | Cash Flow -$3,949 |
|---|---|---|---|---|
| 87.0% | | | $27,829 | |
| Debt Paydown 20.8% | Depreciation 10.5% | | Debt Paydown $6,667 | Depreciation $3,361 |

**Return On Investment Quadrant™ is a trademark of Real Estate Financial Planner LLC

While they are living there, the property has a negative cash-flow. Remember, that's their living expenses. They are living there for just over $300/mo. Their original goal was to reduce their living expenses to $1,000 a month. We beat that by almost $700/mo.!

# Analysis: After They Move Out

Ben and Alyson plan on house hacking one or two more times to help build their rental property portfolio. Once they move out, they will no longer Airbnb the mother-in-law suite to stay compliant with short-term rental rules. It's always a good idea to follow the rules. They'll rent out the main house and mother-in-law suite separately or to a multigenerational family.

| Property Address | Arvada Rental |
|---|---|
| Number of Units | 2 |
| Initial Occupancy Status | Primary Residence |
| | |
| Down Payment Percentage | 5% |
| | |
| Type of Mortgage Insurance | Monthly Paid |

| | | |
|---|---|---|
| Purchase Price | $ | 435,000 |
| Acquisition Costs | $ | 5,697 |
| Loan Costs | $ | 1,540 |
| Down Payment | $ | 21,750 |
| Mortgage Balance | $ | 413,250 |
| Seller Credits | $ | 2,000 |
| Initial Repair Costs | $ | 5,000 |
| Total Initial Investment | $ | 31,987 |

| | |
|---|---|
| Mortgage Interest Rate | 4.500% |
| Mortgage Term (years) | 30 |

Nothing changes on this part of the spreadsheet compared to the previous analysis because they've already purchased the property.

**MONTHLY Rental Income Per Unit AFTER you move out**

| | | |
|---|---|---|
| Unit #1 | $ | 2,100 |
| Unit #2 | $ | 1,000 |
| Unit #3 | $ | - |
| Unit #4 | $ | - |
| **Total Rental Income** | $ | 3,100 |

| | |
|---|---|
| **Vacancy Factor** | 3% |
| **Annual Rent Increase** | 3% |
| **Annual Appreciation Rate** | 5% |
| **Effective Tax Rate** | 25% |

The main house (3/2) should rent for $2,100 to $2,200/mo. The mother-in-law suite should rent between $1000 to $1,100. Both rentals would be long-term. We're using the lower range to be conservative in our analysis.

## Monthly Operating Expenses

| | |
|---|---|
| Do you pay for property management? | No |
| Monthly Reserves for Maintenance - Percentage | 8.0% |
| Is there an HOA | No |

## Additional Annual Expenses

| | | |
|---|---|---|
| Annual Real Estate Taxes | $ | 1,455 |
| Annual Property Insurance | $ | 1,440 |
| Utilities (If paid by owner) | | |
| - Water and Sewer | $ | 672.00 |
| - Trash | $ | 281.00 |
| - Electric | $ | - |
| Landscaping | $ | - |
| Other | $ | - |
| Other | $ | - |

As discussed earlier, the current water bill is lower than expected based on when they bought it, and Ben and Alyson expect the bill to increase to around $1,200/yr. Overall, this number will not have a significant impact on the rent projection. Remember, this is only an estimate to get us in the ballpark.

The tenants will pay the Xcel bill (electric and gas). There is only one gas and electric meter. The owners will most likely put the bill in their name and then prorate the bill back to the tenants. It's a minor inconvenience to bring in extra cash-flow.

| | | | | | | |
|---|---|---|---|---|---|---|
| Total Annual Expenses | $ | 6,824 | | | | |
| Net Operating Income | $ | 29,260 | | | | |
| Less: Annual Mortgage Payments | $ | (25,127) | $413,250 @ 4.500% = $2,093.88 per month | | | |
| Less: Annual Mortgage Payments | $ | (1,777) | Estimated Mortgage Insurance = $148 per month | | | |
| Annual Cash Flow Before Taxes | $ | 2,357 | | | | |

|  | *1st Year Returns* | | | | |
|---|---|---|---|---|---|
| Cash-on-Cash Rate of Return | 7.4% | $2,357 + $31,987 = 7% |
| CAP Rate | 6.7% | $29,260 + $440,000 = 6.7% |
| GRM - Gross Rent Multiplier | 141.9 | $440,000 + $3,100 = 141.9 |

1st Year Return On Investment Quadrant™ (ROIQ)

| Appreciation 68.0% | Cash Flow 7.4% | Appreciation $21,750 | Cash Flow $2,357 |
|---|---|---|---|
| **106.7%** | | **$34,135** | |
| Debt Paydown 20.8% | Depreciation 10.5% | Debt Paydown $6,667 | Depreciation $3,361 |

**Return On Investment Quadrant™ is a trademark of Real Estate Financial Planner LLC

We have an estimated annual cash-flow of $2,357! Hopefully it's a little higher since the lower rent ranges were used. This property is an absolute win because Ben and Alyson dramatically reduced their living expenses while living there and have a positive cash-flowing property after they move out. Remember, the property is underwritten on the conservative side. They may even see better cash-flow. All of this with a 5% down payment that had them all-in for just over $30,000!

This deal analysis is discussed in great detail on episode #148: "Deal Analysis - Arvada Airbnb House Hack" on the Denver Real Estate Investing Podcast.

Also, make sure you read Ben and Alyson's chapter where they discuss operating this house hack. To learn more or to connect with Ben and Alyson, contact them at einspahr22@gmail.com.

If you want to see additional house hacking resources, then check out the Deal Analyses section of the website. The website is updated regularly with recent house hack and Nomad™ case studies.

# Chapter 7

# Personal Finances and Goals

Having a plan for your finances and writing down your investing goals are two key habits that you want to implement. In this chapter we will go over some key points to keep in mind and tips on how to best plan your future, and not only buy your first house hack, but make sure you keep it through the ups and downs of the market, through the curveballs life throws at you and set you up for long term success.

My college degree is in finance, and I love to geek out on numbers. Having your finances in order will help you in blending long- and short-term strategies to create financial wealth through real estate. Below are some examples of how our team can help you do that. One of the unique benefits of working with us is that we incorporate financial modeling and planning with our clients for their real estate investments. This allows us to track and help you towards your retirement cash-flow number.

At the time of writing this chapter, we are currently in a difficult time as each of us is figuring out how to deal with the COVID-19 Pandemic, but I can assure you that our clients who have built up their personal financial foundation are the ones who will weather the storm and are resting much easier than investors who have not.

We have been preaching about this subject for years because it's never a matter of IF there will be a downturn in the market, economic hardship, something happens to your business or in your personal life, or a pandemic but WHEN there will be one.

It's our job to be realistic with you and set you up for success. That means making sure you are good to go when times are good but also means we help prepare you for the bad times. These are the foundational things that you have to make sure you are doing so you can keep the properties you acquire and ultimately set yourself up for long-term wealth.

## Common Principles to Practice:

- Talk with a lender ASAP
    - Know what you can or cannot borrow as it dictates what you can afford.
    - Maybe there's something that needs attention or needs to be fixed before you can qualify. You'll want to take care of that sooner rather than later.
    - Maybe your situation is better than you think, and you can qualify for more or have a better interest rate. You won't know until you have the conversation.
    - It's never too early to talk with a lender. Having your credit pulled will not ruin your life.
    - Are you recording and claiming all rent so we can use that to help you qualify for your loan?
- Down payment and closing costs funds

- ○ House hackers typically need $20,000 to $35,000 in cash to close.

- ○ Are you keeping it in the stock market?
  - ■ Don't lose out on an opportunity because it's in the stock market.
  - ■ If you are ready to buy, move the money to the bank that is not swinging up and down with the market.
  - ■ Have it ready to invest. I keep 100% of my real estate investing money in an Ally savings account.

- ○ Keeping it in bonds?
  - ■ It's not a guarantee to always go up or have the same value.
  - ■ Usually less volatile than the stock market but you have to understand how the bond value changes with the interest rates. Many clients have put money into bonds since they are "safe," but then the interest rate changes and their cash goes down.

- ■ Operating Funds
  - ○ Six months of PITI (Principal, Interest, Taxes, Insurance) and HOA or $10,000, whichever is greater, for EACH property
  - ○ It's smart to have a "catch all" or reserve fund with $10,000 for any miscellaneous expenses for any property (think Murphy's Law.)
  - ○ More cash on-hand makes it easier to weather the storm

- o Good to do an annual review of the accounts to make sure you're still on track

- o How will you fund the next property purchase?

  - Have a plan

  - Good practice to have a separate savings account for this, and when you get to the desired number, you know you're ready to start looking for your next property.

  - Ally.com is a good example of a checking/savings account that is easy to set up and also pays high interest compared to most bonds.

This is not the only way to get your finances in order. It depends, right? If you have another method that works for you, do it! If you want to keep less cash in the bank, and if something major happens, you can pull from your IRA account, great. Just have a plan with liquidity. Set something up that you feel comfortable with and keep some liquid cash in the bank for any "Oh Crap" moments.

It's not worth stretching yourself too thin just to get a deal. As Joe said, "Deals are like busses—another one will be along soon." I always go with the philosophy that I'm not worried about the deal that will "make me." I need to be prepared for the deal that will "break me."

# Four Phases to Investing

I have a four-phase approach to retiring with real estate that I personally use and help clients with.

1. **Your Real Estate Investing Strategy**. You will want to identify what your strategy is. If you don't have a plan, you won't go out and follow it. A simple example of a plan that we've been talking about already: house hacking or Nomading™. For me, it helps to write my strategies and goals down. Instead of doing this on a sticky note, I publish the Denver Real Estate Investing Strategies book every year, and it not only makes me write down my strategy, but holds me accountable to the public, and I like that motivation. If you want to be part of the next book or need help with creating your real estate investing plan, email me at chris@denverinvestmentrealestate.com.

2. **Accumulating Properties.** Once your strategy is in place, it's time to start buying and accumulating properties. For many investors, this is a 10- to 25-year timeline. Most people get rich through real estate slowly. People often ask if they should pay a property off or buy another one. Generally speaking, it's best to focus on accumulating properties before paying them off.

3. **Debt Paydown.** We hear a lot of clients say they have a goal of collecting $10,000 in net rents monthly to use as their passive income. This amount can be greater or smaller depending on your personal situation. Regardless of your goal amount, once you've accumulated enough properties to produce the desired amount of net income, stop accumulating properties and start paying them off. This is known as the debt snowball method. You take the smallest loan balance and pay it off using all the extra cash-flow to prepay the loan. After that one is paid off, repeat the process until all your properties have been paid off.

That is when you can truly count the rental income as passive.

4. **Retirement.** When all the properties are paid off and you are collecting the monthly rents that do not have to be used to pay off any more mortgages, you can use that rental income to help subsidize living expenses.

There is a lot more to creating and executing a plan than the four bullets outlined above, but hopefully it gives you the big picture framework. The majority of investors we talk with have zero framework for a long-term plan. The rest of this chapter will walk you through the basics on creating a plan.

## What is Your Cash-Flow Goal?

To start figuring out your strategy and goal, you must first identify your cash-flow goals.

1. What are your total retirement cash-flow needs?

   o Including social security, pensions, annuities, stocks, bonds, etc.

2. What amount do you need from real estate?

The most common goal we hear from people is $10,000/mo.

## The 33% Rule of Thumb

If your goal is to generate $10,000/mo., will $10,000/mo. in rents suffice? No! Regardless of if the property is paid off or has a mortgage, it has operating expenses. These expenses are what it costs to run the property:

- Insurance
- Taxes
- HOA
- Property management
- Repairs
- Utilities
- Landscaping and snow removal

If you follow BiggerPockets, then you're probably familiar with their 50% rule, which states that 50% of a property's rental income will go towards operating expenses. It may be true in some markets, but not the Denver market. Most of the rentals in Denver run at a 25% to 35% operating expense ratio.

To keep things simple and for quick calculations, we use the 33% rule. Out of every $1 dollar in rental income, $0.33 will go towards operating costs. Is it perfect? It certainly is not, but it's close enough for modeling. **The 33% rule works for long-term rentals as a rule of thumb.** If you're renting room by room or running an Airbnb, you'll have a different number.

**Simple Example to get $10,000/month for retirement:**

$15,000 (gross rents)

-- $5,000 (operating expenses) (⅓ of rents or 33% rule)

-------------------------------------------------------------------

= $10,000 income (paid off properties)

This means that if I'm using the 33% rule and want to have $10,000 cash-flow when I retire, I actually need enough properties to produce $15,000 in gross rents, then start paying off the mortgages. In general, you can usually get to your goal of $10,000 per month faster if you have paid off properties than if you were to accumulate more properties with several mortgages as the mortgages come out of the rents before you get any of that money for yourself.

So, how many properties do you need to retire? Any guesses? The correct answer is… It depends!

Is it a single-family or multi-family? Does it have one bedroom or four bedrooms? In what part of town is it located? What type of rental is it? Each scenario brings in different rental rates. You have to map it out with your personal portfolio. My recommendation is to always use long-term rental rates and averages. It will even out better over the long run and it's better to be conservative and end up happy with more if things are good than overestimate and be disappointed.

Finally, you want to remember that one 20-unit apartment building is very different from one single-family home in terms of cash-flow. Obviously, 20 units will produce more cash-flow than 1 unit. For this reason, we like to focus on a cash-flow goal over the number of properties.

In Denver, rents have generally outpaced the inflation rate. Over the last 40 years, Denver's rents have increased about 4% annually. This is important because $10,000 in 2035 has less buying power than $10,000 today. Following the KISS principle, we can assume that if you buy a rental today, the rents should increase at inflation or slightly higher and give you the same buying power in the future.

# Additional Resources

Creating your strategy, executing it and then achieving your retirement cash-flow is a complicated and lengthy process. This chapter is meant to give you the big picture framework. It's near impossible to teach everything in a book as there are many variables and options that pop up along the way. Later chapters in this book discuss doing cash out refinances and 1031 exchanges that can have a multiplier effect on achieving your cash-flow quicker.

Since creating and achieving your plan is complicated, we meet with clients individually to help map out their investing strategy. We meet with clients on an annual basis to review their portfolio to identify opportunities and make sure they are staying on track with achieving their retirement cash-flow goals. For more details and to schedule an appointment, please visit www.DenverInvestmentRealEstate.com/Consult

# Chapter 8

# Long-Term Modeling for House Hackers

*"In preparing for battle, I have always found that plans are useless, but planning is indispensable."*

### – General Dwight Eisenhower

General Eisenhower's quote sums up the importance of planning and creating a long-term plan. It's absolutely essential to do. You must also realize that what you plan for five years from today is going to change. You will change, the market will change, the lending environment will change, your goals will most likely change and the performance of your rental properties will change—basically, everything will change. One of Joe's favorite quotes sums it up nicely:

*"Everyone has a plan until they get punched in the mouth."*

### – Mike Tyson

As a property investor, you will get punched in the mouth (hopefully only figuratively speaking), and so will your plan. This point is being stressed because many people try to create the perfect plan, which is a waste of time. I say that as someone who has been guilty of that myself.

The goal of this chapter is to walk you through a long-term financial model of buying house hack properties. The model balances key variables and simplicity. It's designed to show you the long-term power of buying multiple house hacks and ask key questions along the way.

# House Hacking Spreadsheet Model

Here's how the spreadsheet model works:

- Buy a property, live there, rent out the bedrooms or other units to live for close to free.

- Two years later, buy a new property, live there, rent out extra rooms to live for close to free. Keep and rent out the previous property.

- Two years later, buy a new property, live there, rent out extra rooms to live for close to free. Keep and rent out the previous property.

- Two years later, buy a new property, live there, rent out extra rooms to live for close to free. Keep and rent out the previous property.

I purposefully made it every two years rather than the required one-year occupancy to show that you don't need to do a perfect execution in order to build long-term wealth. For the sake of simplicity, the model assumes that you're buying the identical property all four times. However, prices, rents, expenses and interest rates all increase.

You can download the House Hacking Spreadsheet at www.DenverInvestmentRealEstate.com/HHSpreadsheet. This is different from Joe's spreadsheet that we shared earlier. Joe's spreadsheet is built more for an individual rental analysis. This spreadsheet is built for long-term modeling. There is a detailed

YouTube tutorial on how to use it. This chapter focuses on the modeling, not the how-to of using the spreadsheet.

# Property #1 Aurora Room by Room Home

Throughout this course, we've referenced the house in Aurora that our client, Austin, is renting out room by room. We'll continue using this property for this scenario. Why? These types of house hacks are readily available. It's not the house hack of the year (those often go to Jeff's extreme house hacking!), but it's a solid, long-term rental that works for the majority of investors.

For this model, we'll use the exact same assumptions from earlier. Here's the spreadsheet again:

| | |
|---|---|
| **Property Address** | Room By Room HH Aurora |
| **Number of Units** | 1 |
| **Initial Occupancy Status** | Primary Residence |
| **Down Payment Percentage** | 5% |
| **Type of Mortgage Insurance** | Monthly Paid |
| **Purchase Price** | $ 375,000 |
| **Acquisition Costs** | $ 7,475 |
| **Loan Costs** | $ 1,540 |
| **Down Payment** | $ 18,750 |
| **Mortgage Balance** | $ 356,250 |
| **Seller Credits** | $ 1,000 |
| **Initial Repair Costs** | |
| **Total Initial Investment** | $ 26,765 |
| **Mortgage Interest Rate** | 3.875% |
| **Mortgage Term (years)** | 30 |

**MONTHLY Rental Income Per Unit AFTER you move out**

| | | |
|---|---|---|
| Unit #1 | $ | 3,200 |
| Unit #2 | $ | - |
| Unit #3 | $ | - |
| Unit #4 | $ | - |
| **Total Rental Income** | $ | 3,200 |

| | |
|---|---|
| **Vacancy Factor** | 5% |
| **Annual Rent Increase** | 3% |
| **Annual Appreciation Rate** | 5% |
| **Effective Tax Rate** | 25% |

## Monthly Operating Expenses

| | |
|---|---|
| **Do you pay for property management?** | No |
| **Monthly Reserves for Maintenance - Percentage** | 8.0% |
| **Is there an HOA** | No |

## Additional Annual Expenses

| | | |
|---|---|---|
| **Annual Real Estate Taxes** | $ | 2,224 |
| **Annual Property Insurance** | $ | 978 |
| **Utilities (If paid by owner)** | | |
| - Water and Sewer | $ | 1,200.00 |
| - Trash | $ | 300.00 |
| - Electric | $ | 1,500.00 |
| Landscaping | $ | - |
| Internet | $ | 600.00 |
| Other | $ | - |

So far, the spreadsheet looks about the same. Once you start buying properties, it'll build out a "Summary" sheet to build out the long-term model. Here's the "Summary" sheet for the first two years of property #1:

| End of Year | Personal Savings | Property #1 | | Total Property Cash-flow | Cash in Savings account | Net Worth |
| | | Cash-flow | Equity | | | |
| --- | --- | --- | --- | --- | --- | --- |
| | | | | | | |
| 1 | $12,000 | 0 | $36,411 | 0 | $12,000 | $48,411 |
| 2 | $12,000 | 0 | $54,662 | 0 | $24,000 | $78,662 |

## Column Descriptions:

**Personal Savings** - Represents the money the client is putting towards their real estate investing savings account. It comes from the reduced living expenses and other money that he can save. For this model, we're assuming he can save $1,000/mo.

**Cash-flow** - Represents the cash-flow from the individual property. In this example, we're using 0. To keep things simple, the personal savings rate was adjusted to account for his minor monthly living expenses.

**Total Property Cash-Flow** - It'll add up the cash-flow from each property to create a total cash-flow.

**Cash in Savings Account** - The total cash in your real estate investing savings account. The amount is calculated from adding the property cash-flow, the personal savings rate and the previous year's balance. When a new property is purchased, the total cash to close is subtracted from this amount.

In the first two years, property #1 is fairly simple, but notice that the net worth and savings account cash are increasing! That's the trend we like to see.

# Property #2: Another Aurora Room by Room Home

To keep things simple, the spreadsheet assumes that he is buying an almost identical house. However, he's buying this in the future, so prices and rents have increased by our assumption inputs. Also, all expenses have increased at a 3% annual inflation rate.

This house now costs $397,838. The good news is that property #1 has seen an equity increase from the appreciation. Now, this second property costs more money; however, the down payment only increases by about $1,142 since he's using another 5% down conventional loan.

By now, you know I like to plan conservatively. The spreadsheet has a variable built-in so you can increase the interest rate percentage between each time you buy the property. In this model, it's assumed the interest rate will increase by 0.5% every time a new property is purchased. Property #1's rate was at 3.875%. Property #2 is at 4.375%. In reality, the last couple of years, we've seen interest rates drop. Again, I always like to plan conservatively.

Here's the summary sheet for property #2:

| End of Year | Personal Savings | Property #1 | | Property #2 | | Total Property Cash Flow | Cash in Savings account | Net Worth |
|---|---|---|---|---|---|---|---|---|
| | | Cash Flow | Equity | Cash Flow | Equity | | | |
| 1 | $12,000 | 0 | $36,411 | | | 0 | $12,000 | $48,411 |
| 2 | $12,000 | 0 | $54,662 | | | 0 | $24,000 | $78,662 |
| 3 | $12,000 | $6,592 | $73,524 | 0 | $38,060 | $6,592 | $14,204 | $125,789 |
| 4 | $12,000 | $7,439 | $93,017 | 0 | $56,865 | $7,439 | $33,643 | $183,525 |

First, look at the "Cash in Savings Account" at years 2 and 3—it goes down. At the end of year 2, you're moving out of property #1 and moving into property #2. The down payment and all the other cash needed to close is coming from the savings account. The table above doesn't show this, but on the spreadsheet, a warning pops up because the $24,000 in the account is less than the total cash of $28,388 needed to close on the property—that's a difference of $4,388.

In reality, that doesn't mean you can't buy it; it means you'll have to pivot with another option. Here are a few things to consider:

- If you're able to increase your personal savings rate.

- The purchase of property #1 included around $3,000 in interest rate buy down. The spreadsheet assumes the same interest rate buydown for property #2. You can skip it.

- We could raise the purchase price by $5,000 and have the seller give you a credit at closing. A credit means the buyer (you) has to bring less cash to the closing table.

- You could wait a couple more months to save the money.

Those are only a few of the options available! To keep things simple in this example, we'll leave it as is.

Look at the cash-flow from property #1 in years three and four. It's pretty damn good around $7,000/yr.! The net worth is now over $100,000. Wow! It's hard to believe, but it's been a very common story in Denver.

# Property #3: Another Aurora Room by Room Home

It's now time to buy house hack #3! To keep things simple, we're assuming that property #3 is just like properties #1 and #2. At the end of year four, it costs $422,066. Since we've left all the assumptions the same, that also means that properties #1 and #2 are worth that much too, which is great news because there is more equity.

It also means that property #3 costs more money. At the end of year four, there is $33,643 in the savings account. You can't see it on the summary page, but the spreadsheet highlights the cell in green because it's more than the total cash needed to close for property #3, which is $30,109. Great!

The spreadsheet is also assuming that the interest rate increases by 0.5% from 4.375% to 4.875%. The increased interest rate increases the monthly mortgage payments.

Let's take a look at the "Summary" sheet results while living in property #3 and renting out #2 and #1 on a room by room basis.

| End of Year | Personal Savings | Property #1 | | Property #2 | | Property #3 | | Total Property Cash Flow | Cash in Savings account | Net Worth |
|---|---|---|---|---|---|---|---|---|---|---|
| | | Cash Flow | Equity | Cash Flow | Equity | Cash Flow | Equity | | | |
| 1 | $12,000 | $0 | $36,411 | | | | | $0 | $12,000 | $48,411 |
| 2 | $12,000 | $0 | $54,662 | | | | | $0 | $24,000 | $78,662 |
| 3 | $12,000 | $6,592 | $73,524 | $0 | $38,060 | | | $6,592 | $14,204 | $125,789 |
| 4 | $12,000 | $7,439 | $93,017 | $0 | $56,865 | | | $7,439 | $33,643 | $183,525 |
| 5 | $12,000 | $8,311 | $113,163 | $5,676 | $76,329 | $0 | $39,815 | $13,987 | $29,520 | $258,828 |
| 6 | $12,000 | $9,209 | $133,985 | $6,574 | $96,476 | $0 | $59,209 | $15,783 | $57,304 | $346,974 |

Look across the row for year 5:

- Property #1 is cash-flowing $9,209 a year!

- Property #2 is cash-flowing $5,676 a year—not bad for just moving out.

- It's over $1,000/mo. in cash-flow from two properties. No one is retiring yet, but it's good cash-flow that is significantly increasing your savings rate.

- The net worth is now over a quarter of a million dollars. Wow!

# Property #4: Another Aurora Room by Room Home

Hopefully, by now, you're realizing the pattern here. It's time to buy property #4, which is similar to the other properties. At the end of year six, there is $57,304 in the savings account. The property costs $447,770 to buy, but because of the power of leverage, only $31,934 cash is needed to close.

In addition to the price increase, all the expenses and rental income has increased as well. Like the other properties, we're adding an additional 0.5% to the interest rate, which now sits at 5.375%.

Let's take a look at the "Summary" sheet results while living in property #4 and renting out the other three properties.

| End of Year | Personal Savings | Property #1 | | Property #2 | | Property #3 | | Property #4 | | Total Property Cash Flow | Cash in Savings account | Net Worth |
|---|---|---|---|---|---|---|---|---|---|---|---|---|
| | | Cash Flow | Equity | Cash Flow | Equity | Cash Flow | Equity | Cash Flow | Equity | | | |
| 1 | $12,000 | $0 | $36,411 | | | | | | | $0 | $12,000 | $48,411 |
| 2 | $12,000 | $0 | $54,662 | | | | | | | $0 | $24,000 | $78,662 |
| 3 | $12,000 | $6,592 | $73,524 | $0 | $38,060 | | | | | $6,592 | $14,204 | $125,789 |
| 4 | $12,000 | $7,439 | $93,017 | $0 | $56,865 | | | | | $7,439 | 33,643 | $183,525 |
| 5 | $12,000 | $8,311 | $113,163 | $5,676 | $76,329 | $0 | $39,815 | | | $13,987 | $29,520 | $258,828 |
| 6 | $12,000 | $9,209 | $133,985 | $6,574 | $96,476 | $0 | $59,209 | | | $15,783 | $57,304 | $346,974 |
| 7 | $12,000 | $10,134 | $155,504 | $7,499 | $117,332 | $4,582 | $79,311 | $0 | $41,685 | $22,216 | $59,585 | $453,416 |
| 8 | $12,000 | $11,088 | $177,745 | $8,453 | $138,923 | $5,535 | $100,148 | $0 | $61,707 | $25,075 | $96,659 | $575,181 |

Look across the row for year eight, your second year of living in property #4:

- The total property cash-flow is $25,075.
- The cash on-hand is close to $100,000!
- The net worth is now over $500,000.

These numbers are starting to look impressive. Remember, it took patience (we're at year eight), the extra management work of self-managing room by room rentals and living with your tenants. Is the sacrifice worth it? It depends, but for most people, the answer is yes.

## The Long-Term Model

At this point, the spreadsheet model assumes that you're done with house hacking. Looking back at the previous "Summary" table, you should have a great foundation laid. In real life, after a few house hacks, most people have "house hack fatigue" and transition to a more traditional investor role. In this situation, you can with the cash-flow, equity and experience that you have gained!

The next "Summary" sheet shows results up to year 40. Spend a few minutes and review the rows for years 10, 20, 30 and 40. Every year, your cash-flow and equity are increasing!

| End of Year | Personal Savings | Property #1 | | Property #2 | | Property #3 | | Property #4 | | Total Property Cash Flow | Cash in Savings account | Net Worth |
|---|---|---|---|---|---|---|---|---|---|---|---|---|
| | | Cash Flow | Equity | Cash Flow | Equity | Cash Flow | Equity | Cash Flow | Equity | | | |
| 1 | $12,000 | $0 | $36,411 | | | | | | | $0 | $12,000 | $48,411 |
| 2 | $12,000 | $0 | $54,662 | | | | | | | $0 | $24,000 | $78,662 |
| 3 | $12,000 | $6,592 | $73,524 | $0 | $38,060 | | | | | $6,592 | $14,204 | $125,789 |
| 4 | $12,000 | $7,439 | $93,017 | $0 | $56,865 | | | | | $7,439 | 33,643 | $183,525 |
| 5 | $12,000 | $8,311 | $113,163 | $5,676 | $76,329 | $0 | $39,815 | | | $13,987 | $29,520 | $258,828 |
| 6 | $12,000 | $9,209 | $133,985 | $6,574 | $96,476 | $0 | $59,209 | | | $15,783 | $57,304 | $346,974 |
| 7 | $12,000 | $10,134 | $155,504 | $7,499 | $117,332 | $4,582 | $79,311 | $0 | $41,685 | $22,216 | $59,585 | $453,416 |
| 8 | $12,000 | $11,088 | $177,745 | $8,453 | $138,923 | $5,535 | $100,148 | $0 | $61,707 | $25,075 | $96,659 | $575,181 |
| 9 | $12,000 | $12,069 | $200,733 | $9,434 | $161,274 | $6,516 | $121,749 | $3,290 | $82,484 | $31,310 | $139,970 | $706,210 |
| 10 | $12,000 | $13,080 | $224,492 | $10,445 | $184,415 | $7,528 | $144,144 | $4,302 | $104,050 | $35,355 | $187,324 | $844,425 |
| 20 | – | $26,551 | $515,011 | $24,009 | $468,306 | $21,191 | $419,338 | $18,070 | $339,463 | $89,821 | – | $1,742,118 |
| 30 | – | $42,596 | $910,223 | $40,054 | $882,718 | $37,236 | $831,345 | $34,115 | $774,841 | $154,001 | – | $3,399,127 |
| 40 | – | $84,262 | $1,223,264 | $84,262 | $1,223,264 | $84,262 | $1,223,264 | $84,262 | $1,223,264 | $337,048 | – | $4,893,057 |

The numbers in year 40 start becoming unbelievable: A house in Aurora will be worth $1.2 million dollars! Remember, this is in future inflated dollars. Throughout my life, I've also talked to a lot of homeowners who bought properties decades ago and for what seemed like an unbelievably low amount. The story that comes to mind is one from a few years ago when I was out walking my dog. It was in a community built in the 1950s. I started talking with an older gentleman who owned his home. Sometime in the 1950s, he purchased it for $14,000. He told me that, back then, it was a lot of money and that he couldn't believe he was spending that much on a home! Now all the houses in the community sell for $750,000 or more.

As you get into the future, what should you do with the properties? Should you start paying down the mortgages? Should you sell and trade-up into bigger properties? As with many answers, it depends! Does the cash-flow from four paid off properties provide you the income that you need? The last chapter of this book will go into detail on what you can do with all the equity that you've earned in the properties.

We covered a lot in the chapter. If you have further questions or need help customizing this to your situation, reach out to us. We're here to help.

# Chapter 9

# Building Your Team

---

As with any real estate investing strategy, it is important to have a solid team in place to help you execute purchasing your real estate properties. The type of investing you are embarking on will dictate who you need on your team. For this section, we will obviously be talking about assembling a team to help you purchase a house hacking property.

## Key People Needed for House Hacking Team:

- Real Estate Agent
- Lender
- Inspector
- Insurance broker

## Real Estate Agent

Every house hack property we have helped our clients acquire—except for one—has been through the Multiple Listing Service (MLS). It's safe to say that if 99% of house hacking deals are found on the MLS, it's a good idea to have a real estate agent working for you. Why? The agent you choose has a fiduciary responsibility to act on your behalf. They have a duty to go to bat for you, have your best interest at heart, make sure you are making wise decisions, protect you, and ultimately, know the ins and outs of the transaction.

Think of your agent as your real estate coach. If you are playing an important game, don't you want a coach in your corner assisting you to a win instead of a referee who's just there to explain the rules, facts and process? You'll be sure to have a better outcome if you have someone "coaching" you through.

As the buyer, you typically will not get a discount by working with the listing agent directly. At most, the selling agent will be a transaction coordinator for you, which means they are not obligated to negotiate and put your best interests first. They are only required to tell you the facts and advise you of your options to move forward. Most selling agents prefer to work with a buyer who is represented with a buyer's agent. If a buyer is unrepresented, it can be a much bumpier road and, ultimately, more work for the listing agent because the buyer most likely doesn't know what they are doing. Another thing to keep in mind is that the commission for the buyer's agent when purchasing a property is usually paid for by the seller.

# What to Look for in an Agent

**An agent who has experience with investment properties.** Even though buying a house hack is buying a primary residence, the analysis is very different when thinking about how the house will perform as a rental property instead of a home that you will live in for several years. Your agent needs to understand the rental and investment worlds as well as have a good understanding of the numbers to make sure it's a good fit for you and your overall investing strategy.

You'll want to make sure that your agent is helping remind you to look at the property through a "rental set of glasses." They need to help you take the emotion out of the transaction and weigh more of how it will perform as a rental.

You'll want to ask how many of the transactions your agent has closed have been on investment properties and, specifically, house hacks. Currently, all of our agents have closed on investment and house hacking transactions, and most are currently house hacking themselves, so we are very familiar with the process and what to look for.

**Does your agent have market knowledge, and are they current with local real estate trends?** It's important that your agent has knowledge of the areas that are transitioning and what areas can bring good values and appreciation. These areas are usually not the same as the highly sought-after neighborhoods where many people choose to live long-term.

Your agent should know which areas have a good price-to-rent ratio and areas that would be most ideal for good living now but also great rental potential later. An example of this would be the Lakewood pockets that are transitioning.

Another example is the Fitzsimons Medical Plaza where they are developing and putting in lots of shops, restaurants and housing that we expect to have greater appreciation in the coming years. You'll want to look for areas known for houses with great layouts for house hacks. There are parts of town where the builders created layouts which are easily turned into mother-in-law suites or have a private entrance.

Knowing where to look to find the right fit is key to making sure you are successful at house hacking and finding renters.

**Does your agent talk to you and educate you on your specific Investor strategy?** Do they have a process to walk you through your investing options and make sure you understand the investing process or your end goal?

The more you can have your strategy dialed in, the easier it will be once you start looking for properties and minimize buyer's remorse.

**Is your agent a full-time Realtor, or do they only do real estate part-time?** Generally speaking, any person who works a job full-time, no matter the profession, is better at that job than a person who only works part-time. A full-time agent has more experience. Experience goes a long way in our current seller's market. More experience will help write more competitive offers and win more properties.

**Can your agent share recent deal analyses on an investment transaction they have completed recently?** What were those numbers like? Knowing the breakdown of transactions your agent closes will help you determine how familiar they are with investing and house hack transactions. If there are no rental properties or house hack deals, that might be a red flag.

**What percentage of your agent's offers for their clients get accepted and go under contract?** On average, how many offers does it take to get an offer under contract? While we don't have official Denver market data, we often hear horror stories of 40 properties toured and 8 offers submitted with nothing under contract. That becomes extremely frustrating and tiresome for anyone looking to invest. We've never had a scenario anywhere close to that.

Our offers get accepted 95% of the time on the first try. Our clients are usually under contract between 1-3 offers. Part of the reason for this is the 16-point checklist we use when writing offers.

**Of the offers that your agent gets accepted, how many of those same deals get to the closing table?** Several deals that go under contract never get to the closing table. They fall out for several reasons, such as lending terms, inspection items or appraisal issues. The average number of transactions in the Denver market that actually make it to the closing table is 78%. Our average is 92%.

**What is the industry reputation of your agent?** We've learned that reputation truly helps you close deals, especially in a seller's market. It's important for the selling side to know that your agent will work hard to get the deal done and represents a qualified buyer.

Throughout the year, we frequently find ourselves in situations like the example below:

We put an offer in on a condo but lost out to a higher priced offer. That deal fell out of contract because the buyer couldn't perform. Seller took another higher offer than ours, which again fell out because the buyer couldn't perform. Selling agent called and said, "We know you have an interested buyer, and we know you will be able to get this deal done and to the closing table. Is your buyer still interested, and can we work with you?" You know you're doing something right when agents call you up to work with you and your qualified clients.

**Does your agent work independently or as part of a team?** The majority of agents are a one man/woman show. Like anyone, we each have our strengths and weaknesses. There are a lot of moving parts of the entire transaction process. Our team focuses on each member's individual strengths and works together to be more efficient and give better service to our clients. Most importantly, our team approach helps us win deals. Period.

Recently, on a Friday morning, we had an investment strategy meeting scheduled with a new client. Preston, Katie and Chris were going to be there. The night before, a closing scheduled for that afternoon got rescheduled for the exact same time. Earlier that morning, one of our clients texted us that they wanted to see a property that morning…at the same time as the rescheduled closing and our new client meeting.

How can an individual agent handle all of that? In reality, they cannot. Since we're a team and everyone is familiar with the process, we were able to divide and conquer.

Preston went to the closing; Katie showed the property, and Chris met with the new client. Not only were we able to get everything accomplished, but it was critical that the property got shown to the client that morning as they are on a very tight timeline with their job relocation that is bringing them to Denver.

The property Katie and the client viewed was a house hack and a great fit for them . Quite a few other buyers thought so too! We knew we had to act fast. Jessica, our transaction coordinator, started drafting up the contract; we reviewed it and then submitted the offer. We knew there were multiple offers on this property.

We recommended our client work with Joe on lending since he has the ability to close in as little as 8 days. Part of the reason we beat out the other offers was because we offered a 12-day close, which is very fast for buying a property with a loan. Since we work as a team and have our processes in place, we were able to execute and get it done.

Speed matters in our current market! There was no way that an individual agent could have handled all of it. This example is fairly common. No matter how well we plan and schedule things out, it's real estate, so curveballs get thrown at us. Our team is structured to handle those curveballs.

# Lender

In all the transactions we have done, we have yet to work with a house hacking client who has gone out and bought a property in all cash. The reason is because it really defeats the purpose of house hacking and using leverage. If you have $400k in cash, you're better off going out and buying a small apartment building than buying a house hack. What makes house hacking so attractive is that you can get the property with as little as 0%-5% down. If you put down very little money, you will need a lender to help with the remaining amount owed.

It's really best to start talking to a lender as soon as possible. A lender's job is to tell you the amount of money that you are truly qualified for, as well as if there are any issues with your credit or something that might make it hard for you to have your loan accepted. The sooner a lender can look at your situation and identify if there will be any issues, the more time you will have to correct any of those issues. For example, what if there is a problem with your credit? Wouldn't you like to know that a few months out so you can correct the issue and get the absolute best rate possible to lend? Or, would you rather be panicked that you only have three weeks to "figure something out" because you waited to talk with a lender until one month before you found a place you wanted to purchase? The buying process is already stressful enough, so do yourself a favor and know where you stand before you start looking.

Ideally, you will want to find a lender who is an investor themselves, or one who at least understands the house hacking strategy. Lending options when house hacking is a bit of a chess game, and the lender needs to make sure this purchase won't hurt your strategy now or in the future.

# What to Look for in a Lender

**Does your lender have experience with investing and house hacking?** Remember, it's a chess game! Make sure your lender is able to look at your future goals and help you make the best decisions based on your investment strategy and long-term goals.

You also want to make sure your lender is talking to you about all your options for down payment and interest rates. If your lender is requiring a 20% down payment on a house hack property, you need to shop around.

The lenders we work with are known for sitting down with clients after they go under contract and give the buyer two to four options on how they can structure their loan. They go over, in detail, how putting more or less money down can change your monthly payment. The same goes for how your interest rate affects your monthly payment and if it would be beneficial to buy your interest rate down.

**Are they a direct lender or a broker lender?** Broker lenders work with several financial institutions, so they will hopefully have several options for you to choose from. The downside could be that each institution might have to pull your credit, which can lead to small credit drops. They may also have additional costs as there are more hands in the pot. A broker might also have access to a lender who offers rare and specialized programs to help buyers get into properties such as first-time buyers programs or income restrictive loans.

Direct lenders cut out all the middlemen and go directly to entities who are lending the money (Freddie Mac, Fannie Mae, Ginnie Mae).

**How does your lender underwrite their pre-approvals?** Joe with Castle & Cooke Mortgage does a full underwriting, which means, if you are pre-approved, all the lender needs are a purchase contract, appraisal and title commitment.

If you are only pre-qualified, you haven't completed the entire process. Pre-approvals are much stronger in the competitive Denver market and more attractive to sellers. In our current market, it's not realistic to submit an offer unless the buyer has been pre-approved.

You should also look for a lender that can help your agent when you put an offer in to assure that listing agent you are qualified to get this deal done and are serious. This reassures the seller that you can get the contract to the closing table and they won't risk falling out of contract over a financing issue.

**Does your lender have in-house underwriting?** Some lenders send files out to a third party to do the underwriting. Some have staff who underwrite in-house, which can lead to being more flexible for certain situations. Lenders who do in-house underwriting usually have better relationships with the people reviewing the files and can get answers quicker than some third parties.

**Does your lender provide updated and clear communication?** No matter how many properties you have bought, the process is always stressful. Joe and Castle & Cooke Mortgage give weekly updates from the time you go under contract, until the day you close.

This helps keep you in the loop and gives you clear expectations for what's coming up. Your lender should also be communicating with your agent to make sure they have all the up-to-date information and can help if the lender is missing something.

It's always a good idea to ask what the "all-in" costs are when you talk to your lender. If they are upfront and straightforward in the beginning, you should expect them to be the same way through the entire process.

**Does your lender have a disaster recovery plan?** Can your lender work remotely so that there's no delay on transactions? The COVID-19 pandemic is a great example. Many lenders couldn't get their clients to the closing table. The lenders we work with, including Joe, were all able to complete the loans and get our clients into homes during an uncertain time.

**What's your lender's track record?** Does your lender fund the loan or drop the ball? The industry average for people who get pre-approved and actually are able to close on their loan is only 78%. That means 22% of people who get pre-approved get turned down by their lender after going under contract. Joe's closing rate is 100%. You can be sure that if Joe says you're pre-approved, there's a 100% chance your loan will close.

# Home Inspector

An inspector is someone you hire once you have a property under contract. The inspector is going to evaluate the property on your behalf. This is someone who is an expert in their field and their full-time job is inspecting homes. The inspector helps you determine if there are any major issues with the house, foundation, roof, appliances,

HVAC systems, sewer line, etc. Don't worry about finding an inspector on your own. Your agent should have several referrals that they can offer you once you are under contract. We have three go-to inspectors that we use on a regular basis for clients and our own investments.

No matter how handy you are, it's always good to get a second pair of eyes and opinion on a multi-hundred-thousand-dollar purchase. This person needs to be someone you trust and has good experience. If you don't have someone you trust, a good resource will be your real estate agent. They usually have a few go-to inspectors they have worked with on past transactions.

# Insurance Broker

It's essential that you have a good relationship with an insurance agent because homeowner's insurance is a requirement by lenders in Colorado. If a lender is going to lend you 95% or even 100% of the money for a house, they want to be sure it is insured in case the house burns down the day after you buy it. The insurance company will pay the money to rebuild it as the lender knows you most likely won't have the money to do so.

If you don't already have a relationship with an insurance agent, again, reach out to your real estate agent or lender as they will have some good resources for you.

Overall, your team will be an essential part of your journey, so you need to make sure you have the right people on the bus! Having an experienced agent and lender to start is key to making sure things go smoothly and you get to the finish line. Having a qualified inspector and knowledgeable insurance agent will help prepare you for long-term planning. As always, it's up to you who you hire to be a part of your team, but the due diligence you put in up front will make for an easier transaction and solid investment.

Below is an example of a pre-approval letter.

# Pre-Approval Letter

**Date: 5/24/2020**

Client Name,

You have provided Lender Name with your documents regarding income sources and assets available to qualify for a residential mortgage loan. Based upon the written information you provided, Lender Name has completed our initial underwriting and has determined that you are eligible for such financing and are approved to meet the financial requirements of the loan.

Please note that a pre-approval notice is not to be construed as a final loan commitment. It is based solely upon the documents you have provided, and your final approval is subject to your appraisal, title commitment and homeowner's insurance. Prior to final approval, Lender Name will complete its final verification of credit, property valuation and stability of assets and income.

Program and funds availability are not guaranteed and are subject to change or termination at any time without advance notice, as determined by investor guidelines, mortgage insurance availability and other factors in the marketplace.

Thank you for choosing Lender Name for your home purchase. I look forward to serving you through this buying experience.

The following terms were discussed with you:

**Sales Price:** $400,000

**Base Loan Amount:** $380,000

**Loan Program:** Conventional 30-Year Fixed

**Property Type:** Single Family Home, Condo or Townhouse

**Loan Term:** 360 months

Sincerely,

**Lender Name**

**Lender Contact Info**

We understand that financing a home is one of the most important decisions a person will make in their lifetime. Loan Officer Name would like to make your experience working with Lender Name as delightful and smooth as possible. Please feel free to call us at: 555-555-5555 if you have any questions on the terms and conditions of this preapproval.

# Chapter 10

# Starting Your Property Hunt

———————◦———————

Going out and actually looking at properties is arguably the most exciting part of the process when searching for homes. While it may be daunting for clients waiting to get to this step, it is important that our clients are fully prepared and knowledgeable about the process. We like to set good expectations so that our clients feel empowered to make quick and knowledgeable decisions.

We've gone over the steps needed to achieve this in our previous chapters, but for sake of review, here's a checklist of what you will want to have reviewed or set in place before you start looking at properties. This foundation will help set you up for success and help execute your goals.

## Checklist

- Pick your agent.
  - Sign the Buyer Agency Agreement. It's a legal document that establishes a fiduciary agreement with the buyer and allows the seller to pay that agent. Basically, it hires your agent as your agent.
- Select your lender.

- ○ Have your pre-approval letter. It's pointless to write an offer without a pre-approval letter in the Denver market as it won't be taken seriously by the seller.

- ○ Pick the lender you're working with because switching lenders during the middle of the transaction can cause issues.

- Know your strategy.
  - ○ You don't need every detail figured out, but have the basics figured out.

- Be smart with your personal finances.
  - ○ Don't buy a car or anything else you would need to finance; it creates more paperwork and could mean you **no longer qualify for the same loan amount.** This may mean that you can no longer close on the property you wanted.

  - ○ Be on credit "lock down" until the transaction is closed. Don't apply for any new credit cards.

- Start property searches and analyses with your agent.
  - ○ Determine criteria and make changes as necessary.

## Our Process for Finding Properties

If you haven't noticed so far, we're very process-driven. In our experience, processes lead to clients being dialed in and ready to go. Plus, it allows us to act very quickly to get properties under contract on your behalf.

# Step #1: Set up Property Searches on REColorado

REColorado is our local MLS. Remember, the vast majority of house hacks are found on the MLS. Zillow and Redfin pull their listings and data from REColorado. REColorado is the source and is where listing agents upload their listings. Zillow and Redfin are great at pulling single-family listings but do a poor job of pulling multi-family data.

REColorado allows us to setup custom searches based on your criteria. These are the searches we typically set our clients with:

- Specific house hacking property searches. These searches—which use a combination of field searching, keyword filtering and square footage requirements—are part of our "secret sauce." They usually find some amazing properties and can avoid hours of scrolling through the MLS!

- Multi-family (2-4 unit) searches. In addition to having accurate data, REColorado will have (if the listing agent uploads it) info on rents, expenses and lease information.

- Custom searches based on the client's needs. We'll create custom searches based on parts of town, commute time, certain features and price point.

# Step #2: Investor Reviews Properties and Sends Over Deal Analyses

Once the property searches are setup, we always have the investor review properties on the MLS and then analyze some deals using Joe's rental property analysis spreadsheet. As we've refined our process, we've noticed a big difference when the client has the ability to underwrite properties compared to us sending over properties. There's a big difference between reviewing a spreadsheet that we prepared versus you having to input the numbers yourself. We want our clients to be educated.

We ask our clients to send over three deal analyses. It doesn't matter how good or bad the deal is. Understanding the process of underwriting the property is the goal.

# Step #3: Review the Deal Analyses

Once the spreadsheets are emailed over, we'll hop on a zoom call or write an email back. It's important to discuss what the client has right, wrong and how we would underwrite the property. Once a client has analyzed a handful of properties, he or she "gets it." It's not rocket science, but it takes a few times to get the hang out of it.

# Step #4: "First Date" Property Walk

Now it's time to walk some properties! This is nicknamed the "first date" property walk because it's meant to help you understand properties from an investor's perspective. Before we walk the properties, we'll underwrite them in the spreadsheet. You are able to compare your spreadsheet to reality and see how different areas and houses compare with how you will balance your investments and personal requirements. Plus, you'll definitely see the power of Photoshop at work when comparing the online photos to real life!

The goal of the "first date" property walk isn't to put an offer in, but it's not uncommon for an investor to submit an offer.

## Step #5: Refine and Keep Looking

Sometimes we put offers in, sometimes we don't. Assuming we don't put an offer in, the next step is refining our property searches based on your feedback. It could be a change in location, property type, bedroom count, size or other variables.

We keep analyzing, walking properties and refining until you're ready to start writing offers. Typically, our clients are ready to put offers in within the first few property tours since they are educated and understand the numbers.

## Structuring Offers

After you go through the process above, you will find a property that fits your criteria and is the one you want to use for your house hack. It's now time to start submitting offers. This is when it gets real. You are signing a contract and putting earnest money into the game.

## Colorado's State Standardized Contract

In Colorado, we're fortunate to have a state standardized contract and other related documents. These are created, approved and updated annually by the Department of Regulatory Agencies (DORA). It allows for quicker and smoother transactions since everyone is using the same forms.

DORA realizes that purchasing real estate is one of, if not the biggest transactions a person has ever made. They don't want prospective buyers to be stuck in a contract with a house that's not the right fit or too expensive. The contract is very buyer friendly. The details are explained in the next chapter, but just understand that it gives the buyer multiple options for terminating the contract.

The contracts are prepared using an online software called CTM eContracts. Fortunately, it allows for electronic signatures for all parties involved.

# What Makes A Good Offer?

It's more than just price! It's common for people to think that the offer with the highest price is the one that always wins. That's not true. There is a lot more to structuring an offer than just having the highest price. We routinely win properties where we are not the highest priced offer.

When drafting and submitting offers, we follow a 16-point checklist:

1. **Establish a relationship with the agent.** Picking up the phone and calling the listing agent is a simple, yet powerful step that many agents skip. The relationship helps understand what the sellers want and helps our offer standout when it's submitted. Rather than just becoming another offer sitting in their email box, the agent associates it with us and what we communicated on the phone call.

2. **Path of least resistance.** After talking with the agent and understanding what they want, we structure our offer to make the path of least resistance for the seller and agent to accept. One example is simply following their submission instructions

of sending it to their correct email address! You would be amazed at how many agents cannot follow instructions. What does that communicate to the other side? If they cannot submit it to the correct email address and follow simple instructions, it communicates that they could be a pain in the butt to work with. There are a lot of little things, but they add up!

3. **Write a detailed cover letter.** When submitting an offer, we always write a concise cover letter that highlights the strength of our offer and how it matches what the seller wants. When agents get over a dozen offers, you want to make it easy for them. This step eliminates the need to dig through our contract for all the details.

4. **Submit a pre-approval letter.** Earlier we discussed pre-approval vs. pre-qualification letters. Pre-approvals show that we are ready to go and have a higher chance of closing.

5. **Source of funds.**

   a. If buying with cash, include source of funds showing the full amount necessary for purchase.

   b. If buying with a loan, include source of funds showing the full down payment already in the bank account.

6. **Call from the lender.** The lender proactively explains that the buyer is qualified, easy to work with, responsive, etc. Plus, the lender can share their experience of working with us. For example, when we submit offers, Joe is copied on the email and immediately follows up with a phone call.

7. **Submit the best financing terms.** Some agents and offers will include options for different lending programs. This communicates uncertainty to the seller. Generally, we have

this determined before the offer and submit with one loan option to show that we are ready to go and using a loan program that is straightforward. Many of the down payment assistance programs come with red tape that can throw uncertainty into the transaction.

8. **Clean and easy-to-read contract.** Structure the offer in a way that is easy to read and understand. If you've received emails or letters where one is confusing and the other is clearly laid out, which one do you pay attention to? The one that is easy to read! Listing agents and sellers are like other people—they are busy! Let's not make it harder for them to understand our contract. Many agents add custom clauses when the contract already has it in there. Don't add unnecessary or repetitive language!

9. **Early buyer termination dates.** As mentioned earlier, the Colorado contract is very buyer-friendly. It's best to put the most common dates and deadlines that buyers terminate on early rather than later. We always recommend our clients hire a home inspector. The inspection is what causes many deals to fall apart. Rather than having our inspection objection and resolution deadlines three weeks after going under contract, we often have it seven days out. It gives us and our client plenty of time to do our due diligence (don't worry, if we need more, we can push the dates out) and lets the seller know that we're moving fast. It's in everyone's best interest to know sooner rather than later if we're moving forward or terminating.

10. **Limited inspection.** You would be surprised at some of the small and unimportant items that buyers will ask sellers. The inspection objection is not where you nitpick over small items such as door stops or paint colors! We let the seller know that

we're not going to nitpick over small items, which is often a huge relief to them.

11. **Unusual price offer.** Many people round to whole numbers, such as $340,000. We'll often write offers at a unique price like $341,100 for example. It helps our offer stand out and lets the seller know we put thought into calculating it. Plus, sometimes we've won some offers just because we were the highest by a couple hundred dollars!

12. **Escalation clause.** Sometimes we will add an escalation clause to the contract, which tells the seller we'll raise the purchase price up to a certain amount to beat out other offers. We require the listing agent to send us a copy of a bona fide offer to make sure it's legit.

13. **Rush the appraisal.** If closing quickly is important to the seller and will help us win the deal, we can write the offer so we can close in 10 days. We're able to do that because we work with great lenders, such as Joe, who can act fast and rush an appraiser out to the property. It'll cost you a few extra hundred dollars, but if that is what helps us win the deal, then a few hundred dollars is inconsequential.

14. **Flexible closing date.** If you're buying the house from an owner-occupant, they are often selling their property and buying a new one. They are running into the same issues that other buyers are and may miss out on a few properties. If we can offer a flexible closing date, that can be a huge relief to them. For my primary residence that I purchased, the sellers were waiting for their new-build home to be completed. Builders are notorious for pushing back closing dates. I gave my sellers the option to push our closing date back if they needed. They avoided a lot of stress and the potential headache

of moving twice and staying in a hotel for a week or two. Additionally, if an investor is selling the property and are in a 1031 exchange, a flexible closing date is highly desirable for them too.

15. **Seller leaseback.** Sometimes sellers need to close by a certain date but want or need to remain in the property. They essentially become tenants. Again, this is like the example above where it can make their life a lot easier and less stressful. These are usually for short-term situations, or less than 60 days.

16. **Backup offers.** More than 20% of all properties in Denver fall out of contract. Some go back to the MLS, some do not. If our offer loses out, we always ask the agent about submitting a formal backup offer or let them know to call us if anything doesn't work out. Guess what? We win quite a few places like this!

Are any of these points the "magic bullet" that always helps us win? No. The combination of them, along with our reputation, helps win quite a few and a higher percentage than the average Denver agent. Becoming a real estate agent has a relatively low barrier to entry: a person has to take some classes and spend a few hundred dollars to take an exam, which is not too hard to pass. The classes and the exams, like a lot of schools, don't teach practical real-world tips like our checklist. Our offers often stand out compared to other ones, which helps us win them!

# Submitting an Offer

Now it's time for us to submit the offer on your behalf! As you can tell, the prepping and structuring of the offer takes time, whereas submitting it is fairly straightforward. We'll go through common questions from clients:

**"Does it cost money to submit an offer?** No, it doesn't cost anything to submit an offer.

**"How soon will we know?"** The Denver market moves fast, so we usually know within 24 to 48 hours.

**"What are the outcomes after we submit the offer?"** There are three:

1. Reject - Offers have an acceptance deadline, so the listing agent can verbally say, "We are not accepting this offer," or, if you haven't heard anything from the listing agent before the acceptance deadline, the offer expires and is officially rejected.

2. Counter - A negotiation where seller says, "Yes, we like the offer, but we need to address a few small changes."

3. Accept – The offer is good, seller signs and property is officially "Under Contract!"

Jeff, who has been through this process several times, reiterates how having a good team in place is really key to understanding the process of looking at properties and, ultimately, finding the right property for you. The more you understand the process and have a team that has your back and is willing to go to bat for you, the greater your chances are for getting the property you want under contract in a competitive market such as Denver's.

Building your team is arguably one of the most important steps in any investing strategy. We work with investors, lenders, inspectors and other teams of real estate professionals on a daily basis. We would love the opportunity to help you with any needs you have. If you have questions, need clarification, or would like to set up a consultation with our team, please contact us at Chris@DenverInvestmentRealEstate.com or visit our website www.denverinvestmentrealestate.com/

# Chapter 11

# You're Under Contract

———————— o ————————

Congratulations! You are under contract. Now that you've identified a great property and are officially under contract, we want to talk about the next steps. We'll discuss your responsibilities, our responsibilities and what you can expect moving forward.

The information below is going to be detailed but note that you should use this as a reference. Don't get caught up on too many specifics now because we will go over each of these steps once you are under contract. We will also send out an email for the next steps, which will help you know what to focus on. Hold on to your hats, the next steps happen pretty quickly.

## Next Steps:

1. **Activity/Deadline Calendar** - The online contract software generates a calendar that you can sync with your current calendar. It lays out what items are coming up and when they are due. Helps clients follow along and always know where we are in the transaction/process.

2. **Earnest Money** - This is usually about $3k-$10k and is submitted with a personal check, wire transfer or smartphone app. You will know the amount before you go under contract. This is "good faith" money that will be used towards your

down payment, unless you terminate the contract appropriately, in which case you will get this money back. If you do not terminate the contract appropriately, you could lose the money. It's usually the first thing that will be outlined in the activity calendar as it's usually due within three days of the offer being accepted. It's typically deposited with the title company. The earnest money solidifies the contract as being accepted, active and in full force.

3. **Lending** - Your agent should always send an executed contract to the lender so they know it's time to start finalizing everything on their end. The executed contract allows the lender to calculate the interest rate options, PMI options and closing costs. You'll sit down with your lender to go over various scenarios. Make sure you do this as soon as possible!

4. **Inspection** - We usually schedule the inspection to take place within three to seven days of going under contract. Scheduling it ASAP is in everyone's best interest. Once we have videos and reports back from the inspector, we will review the property again and prepare an inspection objection or have a professional (roofer, HVAC, Plumber) check any issues. We also re-run the numbers to make sure it still makes sense as a rental.

   There might be something that needs time to fix, and you want to have as much time as possible to allow industry professionals to rectify any problems and negotiate those with the seller. The quicker items get addressed, the better chance you have at staying on track with your activity deadlines.

   o We recommend that house hackers hire a home inspector, conduct a sewer scope and complete a radon test. While these three items will cost you between $500-$800 out-of-pocket, this is money well spent for due diligence on a $400,000 purchase. Spending that money is miniscule compared to having to replace a $15,000 sewer line a few weeks after closing.

- **Overall Home Inspection.** This is done by a third party who will walk the property and send you a detailed report. This will cost between $300-$500. We highly recommend that you attend your inspection to talk with the inspector and really learn the property.

- **Sewer Scope.** This is done by a third party who puts a camera down the sewer line to see if there are any major cracks, blockages or tree roots intruding into the line, which could cost thousands if they are not addressed timely. Many of the properties we buy were built in the 50s and 60s and have clay sewer pipes. It's very common to have root intrusion and other line issues. This should cost between $100-$150.

- **Radon test.** Radon is a colorless, odorless, radioactive gas that is very common in Colorado and is a health and safety concern. Long-term exposure can lead to long-term health issues. If there are high levels of radon, installing a radon mitigation system is a relatively easy fix and costs around $1,000. The cost for the radon test is between $100-$150.

5. **Insurance** - Reaching out to your insurance agent will be another task that is a high priority. The insurance company will need to communicate with your lender as well as check into any claims previously made on the house. What if there's

an outstanding roof claim, or you're located in a flood zone? You want to be sure you know any and all issues so you have the right coverage and don't get caught with any old baggage. Insurance is required by lenders and needs to be in place by closing.

6. **Appraisal** - This is ordered by your lender and is completed by a third party to get the value of the property to make sure the lender isn't over-lending on the property. This can be one of the bigger hurdles that will determine if your loan can be approved or not. The lender usually orders it right away in case there are any issues with the appraisal. Note that just because you put in an offer "over asking" doesn't necessarily mean it's over the valued price. The majority of property appraisals come in at value or above. We have low appraisal issues with less than 5% of our properties under contract. Appraisals typically cost $600 ($625 if FHA loan) for a single-family home, $800 for a multi-family home, and $700 if it's an investment property.

   ○ One strategy to have a more competitive offer might be to "rush" the appraisal. It will cost an additional $600 approximately, but it could be something that sets you apart from other offers as it allows for a quick closing within 10 days. We'll use this when speed matters and we're up against cash offers.

7. **Closing** - The closing is where you sign a lot of paperwork and officially become the owner of the property! Closings typically take place at a title company.

# Dates and Deadlines

This next section discusses section 3. Dates, Deadlines and Applicability of the contract. Don't worry about understanding all of the details in this book. When the time comes to put in offers, we'll walk you through all the dates. Below is a screenshot of that section of the contract. The right-hand column will have actual dates when you're under contract. For this example, we're putting in the typical time frame of when the deadline is.

MEC stands for "mutual execution of contract." You'll sign the offer before we submit it. It becomes an executed contract once the seller signs it. If you sign the offer on a Monday and the seller signs on a Tuesday, then it's mutually executed on Tuesday. Look at the example for item number #1, "Alternative Earnest Money Deadline" below. Our notes say, "2 to 3 days after MEC." Assuming the contract is executed on Tuesday, it'll be two or three days after Tuesday when the earnest money is due. Again, don't get hung up on the specifics, just get the gist.

**3. DATES, DEADLINES AND APPLICABILITY.**
    **3.1.   Dates and Deadlines.**

| Item No. | Reference | Event | Date or Deadline |
|---|---|---|---|
| 1 | § 4.3 | Alternative Earnest Money Deadline | 2 to 3 days after MEC |
| | | **Title** | |
| 2 | § 8.1, § 8.4 | Record Title Deadline | 7 days after MEC |
| 3 | § 8.2, § 8.4 | Record Title Objection Deadline | 10 days after MEC |
| 4 | § 8.3 | Off-Record Title Deadline | 7 days after MEC |
| 5 | § 8.3 | Off-Record Title Objection Deadline | 10 days after MEC |
| 6 | § 8.5 | Title Resolution Deadline | 14 days after MEC |
| 7 | § 8.6 | Right of First Refusal Deadline | N/A |
| | | **Owners' Association** | |
| 8 | § 7.2 | Association Documents Deadline | 7 days after MEC |
| 9 | § 7.4 | Association Documents Termination Deadline | 10 days after MEC |
| | | **Seller's Disclosures** | |
| 10 | § 10.1 | Seller's Property Disclosure Deadline | 3 days after MEC |
| 11 | § 10.10 | Lead-Based Paint Disclosure Deadline | 3 days after MEC |
| | | **Loan and Credit** | |
| 12 | § 5.1 | New Loan Application Deadline | 2 days after MEC |
| 13 | § 5.2 | New Loan Termination Deadline | 5 days before closing, talk w/ lender |
| 14 | § 5.3 | Buyer's Credit Information Deadline | N/A |
| 15 | § 5.3 | Disapproval of Buyer's Credit Information Deadline | N/A |

| 16 | § 5.4 | Existing Loan Deadline | N/A |
|---|---|---|---|
| 17 | § 5.4 | Existing Loan Termination Deadline | N/A |
| 18 | § 5.4 | Loan Transfer Approval Deadline | N/A |
| 19 | § 4.7 | Seller or Private Financing Deadline | N/A |
| | | **Appraisal** | |
| 20 | § 6.2 | Appraisal Deadline | 14 - 21 days after MEC, consult w/ lender |
| 21 | § 6.2 | Appraisal Objection Deadline | 14 - 21 days after MEC, consult w/ lender |
| 22 | § 6.2 | Appraisal Resolution Deadline | 14 - 21 days after MEC, consult w/ lender |
| | | **Survey** | |
| 23 | § 9.1 | New ILC or New Survey Deadline | 14 - 21 days after MEC |
| 24 | § 9.3 | New ILC or New Survey Objection Deadline | 14 - 21 days after MEC |
| 25 | § 9.3 | New ILC or New Survey Resolution Deadline | 14 - 21 days after MEC |
| | | **Inspection and Due Diligence** | |
| 26 | § 10.3 | Inspection Objection Deadline | 7 days after MEC |
| 27 | § 10.3 | Inspection Termination Deadline | 10 days after MEC |
| 28 | § 10.3 | Inspection Resolution Deadline | 10 days after MEC |
| 29 | § 10.5 | Property Insurance Termination Deadline | 14 days after MEC |
| 30 | § 10.6 | Due Diligence Documents Delivery Deadline | 7 days after MEC |
| 31 | § 10.6 | Due Diligence Documents Objection Deadline | 10 days after MEC |
| 32 | § 10.6 | Due Diligence Documents Resolution Deadline | 14 days after MEC |
| 33 | § 10.7 | Conditional Sale Deadline | N/A |
| 34 | § 10.10 | Lead-Based Paint Termination Deadline | 7 days after MEC |
| | | **Closing and Possession** | |
| 35 | § 12.3 | Closing Date | 30 days after MEC |
| 36 | § 17 | Possession Date | Day of closing, unless PCOA or tenants |
| 37 | § 17 | Possession Time | After delivery of deed and loan funding |
| 38 | § 28 | **Acceptance Deadline Date** | 24 hours |
| 39 | § 28 | **Acceptance Deadline Time** | |

1. **Alternative Earnest Money Deadline** - date the earnest money needs to be delivered to the title company

**Title Items** - The title company will initiate and pull these records for the buyer, then provide the buyer with results of what was found for them to review. It can expose any liens or judgements put on the property by the seller. These documents will also be sent to the lender who needs to double check that there are no additional liens, judgements or bankruptcies that would be ahead of the new mortgage if they were to lend money.

2. **Record Title Deadline** - Date title company is required to provide the buyer with an initial title commitment.

3. **Record Title Objection Deadline** - Date buyer has to respond to the seller if there are any issues with the title.

4. **Off-Record Title Deadline** - Date title company is required to provide the buyer with a list of items that might not pull up

in a normal title search or haven't been officially recorded with the county but items that the seller is required to disclose.

5. **Off-Record Title Objection Deadline** - Date the buyer has to respond to seller if there are any issues with items not recorded with the county.

6. **Title Resolution Deadline** - Date all negotiations between buyer and seller need to be resolved with a plan in place as to how to move forward with fixing any title issues if necessary.

7. **Right of First Refusal Deadline - N/A**

**Owner's Association** - Listing agents may have info on how to obtain these or they can be ordered by the title company. We want to see the status and "health" of the homeowner's association (HOA) if one is present (meeting minutes, financial statements, guidelines and regulations). The buyer is not able to object to anything of the HOA, but they can terminate the contract if they don't feel comfortable purchasing a property under that HOA. Note that the HOA will not change anything based on your preference, which is why you are allowed to terminate the contract if the HOA doesn't fit your goals. For example, if the HOA does not allow long- or short-term rentals in the community.

8. **Association Document Deadline** - Date association documents are required to be delivered to the buyer for review.

9. **Association Documents Termination Deadline** - Date by which buyer may terminate the contract if they find something in the documents provided that would cause major concern in purchasing the property.

**Seller's Disclosures** - In Colorado, sellers are required to disclose any known material facts that might affect the property.

10. **Seller's Property Disclosure Deadline** - Date by which seller must fill out any known facts about the property and deliver to the buyer (known roof replacement, water damage, structural issues, electric rewire, etc.)

11. **Lead-Based Paint Disclosure Deadline** - If the property was built before 1978, there is a chance that lead-based paint was used. This form is from the seller to the buyer stating whether or not the seller knows if any lead-based paint was used in or on the house. Buyer has the right to test the property for lead-based paint.

**Loan & Credit** - While you have a pre-approval, there are more steps required by the lender to fully approve your application now that you have identified a property.

12. **New Loan Application Deadline** - Date by which you need to have sat down with your lender and gone over all your options and decided on a course of action to go through with the loan for that specific property.

13. **New Loan Termination Deadline** - Usually the last opportunity to get out of the contract and get your earnest money back if something dire happens like you lost your job during the time you've been under contract, or you bought a new car and no longer qualify for the loan.

14. **Buyer's Credit information Deadline** - Date by which you must get all your information to your lender regarding credit and lift any freezes so the lender can accurately qualify you.

15. **Disapproval of Buyer's Credit Information Deadline** - If you have an issue with what was found on your credit report or disagree with something on your credit report, this is the date you can object to that.

16. **Existing Loan Deadline** - Only applies if you are taking over an existing loan. Not very common, but if it occurs, this is the date you have to determine that.

17. **Existing Loan Termination Deadline** - If you don't like the terms of taking over an existing loan or you can't qualify, this is an opportunity to get out of the contract and get your earnest money back. Again, it's not common.

18. **Loan Transfer Approval Deadline** - Date by which the existing loan would need to be transferred into your name and you assume responsibility for the loan.

19. **Seller or Private Financing Deadline** - If the seller is giving you a loan or if there is another individual who is giving you some of the money required to buy the property (not including down payment), there is another process with that. This is the date all that paperwork is required to be completed. This is also uncommon.

**Appraisal** - A key piece for the lender to let them know how much the property is worth and determines if they can lend you all of the money needed for the transaction.

20. **Appraisal Deadline** - Date by which you need to have completed the appraisal.

21. **Appraisal Objection Deadline** - Date by which the buyer can go back to the seller and ask for more money if the appraisal doesn't come back or is greater than the contract price. For

example, you are under contract on a property for $400k, but the appraisal comes back at $390k. You can ask the seller to lower the purchase price to $390k, terminate the contract or increase your down payment. It's common for buyers and sellers to split the difference.

22. **Appraisal Resolution Deadline** - If there is an objection from the buyer on the purchase price based on the appraised value, there will be a negotiation period between buyer and seller to work out a solution. This is the date that resolution needs to be submitted in writing.

**Survey** - Buyer always has the right to do a survey of the land associated with the property through an Improvement Location Certificate (ILC), which is a mini survey and will show the boundaries and lot lines of the property as well as any easements. You can also request a full survey.

23. **New ILC or New Survey Deadline** - Date by which the new survey or ILC needs to be completed.

24. **New ILC or New Survey Objection Deadline** - Date to let the seller know that the buyer has an issue with something that was found in the survey or ILC. For example, if a newly-built garage encroaches on the neighboring property by two feet.

25. **New ILC or New Survey Resolution Deadline** - Date all negotiations need to be completed by between the buyer and the seller to find a solution and move forward with the transaction.

**Inspection & Due Diligence** - Time to find out any major issues with the property that might change a buyer's mind if they want to follow through with the purchase.

26. **Inspection Objection Deadline** - Date by which a buyer needs to let the seller know all the terms they want to negotiate or issues that need to be fixed before the purchase is complete.

27. **Inspection Termination Deadline** - The buyer has the option to terminate the contract and get their earnest money back as long as they terminate the contract in writing by this date.

28. **Inspection Resolution Deadline** - Date by which the buyer and seller end negotiations and determine a solution for all issues in the inspection objection to move forward with the transaction.

29. **Property Insurance Termination Deadline** - Date by which the buyer can terminate the contract and get their earnest money back if they are not comfortable with the terms of the insurance or there are any adverse effects of the insurance. For example, if the insurance company cannot insure the property or it's in a flood zone that raises the premium higher than you expected.

30. **Due Diligence Documents Delivery Deadline** - Date by which the seller must provide all documents to the buyer so they can accurately do their due diligence on the property (ex. appliance warranties, previous appraisals, receipts or permits for newly-rehabbed items on the property).

31. **Due Diligence Documents Objection Deadline** - The buyer must deliver to the seller any items that they want further information on.

32. **Due Diligence Documents Resolution Deadline** - Date by which the buyer and seller must come to an agreement on a solution for any issues brought up in the objection. If no solution is made by this date, the transaction self-terminates.

33. **Conditional Sale Deadline** - This is the last date a buyer is able to back out of the contract if they need to sell their current property before purchasing the property in this transaction.

34. **Lead-Based Paint Termination Deadline** - Date by which the buyer can terminate the contract if they are worried about the amount of lead-based paint that is in/on the property.

**Closing and Possession** - Plan as to when the purchase is finalized, and the buyer officially becomes the new owner!

35. **Closing Date** - When the transaction expects to close.

36. **Possession Date** - Date when the buyer gets the keys and can officially walk into their new home. Many times, this is the same day as closing, as long as there is no agreement that the sellers will stay in the property longer. Also, any leases that are currently in place will supersede the possession date.

37. **Possession Time** - Time of day when the buyer gets the keys and can officially move in or take possession of the property.

38. **Acceptance Deadline Date** - Date by which the seller needs to let the buyer know if their original offer has been accepted. If there is no communication by this date, it is assumed that the offer has NOT been accepted. Typically, it's 24-48 hours after the offer is submitted to allow the seller time to review and decide if they want to accept the offer.

39. **Acceptance Deadline Time** - Time of day when the seller needs to let the buyer know if their original offer has been accepted.

Overall, these dates and deadlines can change and be negotiated on with good communication from the real estate agents on both sides of the transaction. Typically, in Colorado, this is about a 30-day process.

Again, there are a lot of details, so it's ok if you don't understand or follow everything right now. We will hold your hand through this process. If you need time to think or fix something, we can push these dates to get things resolved.

If you have any questions, please reach out.

# Chapter 12

# Just Closed, Now What?

So, you finally found a great property that will work for you, and the keys are in your hands. What a wonderful feeling! Now what? This is where the fun starts! In this chapter, our expert House Hacking Coach, Jeff White, will guide you through the top six things you must consider before acquiring your first tenant.

## Fair Housing Laws

It's important for you to understand and abide by applicable federal, state and local fair housing laws in order to run a compliant real estate business. **Disclaimer: The advice in this chapter is NOT legal advice. Always consult with the appropriate professional.**

### The Basics of Fair Housing Laws

- Federal laws are in place that grant fair housing protections to renters from being discriminated against when applying for housing. The federal law prohibits discrimination against an applicant based on their race, color, religion, gender, national origin, familial status, or physical or mental disability.

- State and Local law - Each may have additional protected classes; for example, veteran or military status, criminal history, gender identity expression, etc. You need to be aware of these classes for each city and county you have a property in.

- "Mrs. Murphy" Exemption - This exemption provides that, if you are living in a property as your primary residence with four or fewer rental units, that property is exempt from the Fair Housing Act. "Mrs. Murphy" is the hypothetical elderly widow who is supplementing her limited income by renting a portion of her home and has a say in who she chooses as her tenant(s). Keep in mind, the exemption does not apply to rental advertising.

  - Example: If a 25-year-old female was house hacking and only wanted other female roommates or only roommates who were around her same age, she could deny any male applicants who were 40+ years old, and she would be within her rights. She would not be violating any Fair Housing Laws.

  - Remember, the information given does not constitute legal advice. You should talk to a lawyer and make sure that the "Mrs. Murphy" exemption is recognized in the city or county you will be residing in before you exercise it.

  - If you are a real estate professional or own multiple properties, there may be some additional stipulations for this exemption as well.

# Advertising Your Property

Once you are familiar with the Fair Housing Laws for your specific city and county, you are ready to create an advertisement to fill the vacancy. Properly marketing your rental property is an important part of finding reliable and high-quality tenants. Without good advertising, it's difficult to generate enough interest in your rental, and the longer a rental property sits empty, the more you lose.

**The 3 Key Elements of a Good Property Advertisement:**

- Pictures are valuable
  - Renters look at pictures first before reading an entire listing. Having five to ten high-quality pictures goes a long way because they can justify a higher rent price, which can help you rent your unit faster.
  - Don't hold back from light staging (artwork, area rugs, accessories, etc.) because empty units can take longer to rent. The more you can convey a sense of an inviting home, the more interest you get and the faster you will rent the property.
  - Consider hiring a professional real estate photographer to take pictures for you because it ensures the absolute best quality since their wide-angle lens will be able to capture more of the space and details.
  - If permission is granted, use the pictures from the listing. You must get permission from the listing agent and/or seller to use the photos so you don't violate any copyright issues.

- Effective Property Description
  - Keep the property description short and sweet (1-2 short paragraphs) in order to significantly increase the amount of inquiries. The goal is to get prospects to engage!
  - Include descriptive information renters immediately want to know about the property. Mention appealing amenities, available date and highlights of what's nearby like schools, restaurants, shops, parks, etc.
  - Check out other listings to see what seasoned landlords and property managers are highlighting—and what they are leaving out. People are looking for a place to call home, so eliminate anything that doesn't entice the prospect to want to reach out.
  - Your number-one goal is to attract the most prospective tenants.
- Advertising Your Property
  - The more exposure the better! There are many listing platforms available on the market, so how will you know where to spend your time? Consider trying the options listed below. Remember, the more inquiries you can get, the better your pool for screening and finding a high-quality tenant.
  - Facebook Marketplace is my top recommendation because it expands your reach and puts your unit in front of more potential tenants than industry websites alone. In my experience, it has rendered the most interest with the least amount of work.

o Zillow is the highest rated rental listing site, and it also posts to Trulia and HotPads, creating a huge opportunity for visibility and more exposure.

o Room rental platforms such as Roomster, Roomies and Cozy.co are great for finding a roommate.

o Avoid Craigslist! There are too many risks for landlords these days. It used to be decent, but not anymore. It's overrun by scammers.

# Getting Your First Tenant

Ok, so the text messages, phone calls and social media messages are rolling in because you have an amazing advertisement that has attracted lots of interest. Congrats! How do you decide which tenant to rent to? It's too soon to know, but so far, you're on the right track.

**Four important steps to ensure a smooth rental process:**

- Showing Your Property to Potential Tenants
  o The best times to schedule a showing are evenings (after work) on weekdays, and 12pm-2pm or 1pm-3pm on weekends. Be flexible for those who may work nights or weekends.

  o Don't post your property and postpone showings until five days later; you will lose highly-motivated applicants.

  o Group Showing vs. Individual Showings – Don't waste your time with individual showings (one time slot per person). Schedule 10-15 people in a two-hour window since you will experience a high "no show" rate—about 50%, even with confirmation.

- o If you have more than one prospective tenant at the showing, it creates a sense of urgency to fill out an application because they will see other people are interested too.

- Tenant & Credit Screening to Protect Your Property
  - o Reduce your liabilities by uncovering criminal history of property damage, violent offenses and other serious crimes that can be a risk to your property and your tenants by carefully screening prospective tenants carefully.

  - o Avoid any question of discrimination if all your applicants use the same third-party system to apply.

  - o There are some great websites that will take care of the screening process for you, and you get to set the standards for what you use to accept/not accept.

    I use and recommend Cozy.co because it reveals bankruptcies, sex offender lists, evictions, judgements, etc. It also performs soft credit pulls, so it won't mess up any lending qualifications for future tenants.

  - o Application Fee – By using Cozy.co, the application fee is paid to a third-party system, so you won't have to worry about potential tenants wondering if you made money on their application because landlords are removed from the process.

  - o Cozy.co emails you letting you know that it has completed the application, and you get results within minutes.

- Assessing a tenant's ability to effectively pay the rent, aka underwriting

  o Never overlook or rush this step just to fill a vacancy; it's a worthwhile step.

  o Have a diligent underwriting process, even if it takes a little more time upfront to land a qualified tenant. Check judgements, ensure they have a 3x rent-to-income ratio, verify paystubs, call at least two prior landlords, and ask questions to help you make a better-informed decision.

  o Ask every landlord the same questions. References from past landlords are more forthcoming and can indicate how the potential tenant might treat your property, if they will pay their rent on-time and the likelihood of receiving noise complaints from neighbors, etc.

  o When it comes to hard financial times (much like the pandemic we are currently in), it's the landlords who took the time to underwrite their tenants properly who will be sleeping easy because their tenants were able to pay rent.

- Accepting or Rejecting a Prospective Tenant

  o As a landlord, you have the freedom to choose the "most qualified applicant." If you have two very qualified tenants, make your choice on a first-come-first-serve basis to save yourself from any discrimination claims.

  o You must tell the prospective tenant why they did or didn't get approved for the property via email or a written letter (no text or phone calls). As long as the reason for rejection is legitimate and meets Federal Fair Housing Guidelines, you can say "no" to the applicants that you won't be accepting.

o   Remember to always keep correspondence in writing.

o   For highly qualified applicants who didn't quite make the cut, gently decline the applicant with the following example: "Thank you for applying, we've accepted someone who is a little better fit for the unit, but if we have another property become available, we will let you know as you were a highly-qualified prospective tenant."

# Lease Signing

Hire an attorney to draft a good, strong lease for you. Avoid quick one-pagers or a generic lease you found on the internet that may not factor in local and city laws or critical clauses. You need to protect yourself, and it's always better to have a lease that covers too much rather than not enough. If things go south with a tenant, the lease is what will help you get the non-compliant tenant out and save you from lawsuits.

**Consider these five main concepts to avoid pitfalls**

- Lease Structure
   o   Be extremely specific about the space intended for the tenant and where they can/can't put their stuff (rooms, common areas, storage spaces, garage, whole unit, etc.). To avoid disputes, it is better to be more detailed than vague. Mention that drawers will be assigned and labeled in the kitchen and bathrooms if you rent by the room.

- Setting House Rules
  - Include detailed house rules like quiet hours, lawn care, guests, smoking, etc. Include designations, like who is responsible for lawncare, snow removal, trash, etc. When you have a strong, detailed lease, you won't be seen as the "bad guy" if you have to evict a tenant for violating the lease or any of its provisions.

  - Print the house rules on a separate document making it easy for them to refer to it since most people never read the lease thoroughly. This gives you a chance to emphasize the importance of the house rules.

- Start with a Shorter Lease Length
  - Start with a six-month lease and include a security deposit amount. Sometimes, shorter can be better when renting room-by-room as it gives you a "test drive" or a "feel" for the other person before committing to a one- or two-year lease and vice versa for the tenant.

  - In Colorado, it's in your best interest to end a lease between April and September as that is the prime time for people moving, which gives you the best chance to quickly replace a tenant with a new one and avoid any vacancy. When leases end in the middle of winter or around holidays, it takes longer to rent or lower prices to fill vacancies.

- In-Depth Lease Signing Appointment
  - Go over the entire lease thoroughly. Read every word and re-emphasize addendums such as drug use and tobacco, which will set expectations upfront and avoid

misunderstandings. Be clear about the boundaries and expectations of the guest policy. Also, be upfront about enforcing these boundaries.

o   Breaking the lease is a serious matter, so avoid this sticky situation by discussing clauses and how failure to comply can be grounds for eviction.

- Separating Out Utilities

o   Using the bill-back method may seem easy enough but avoid it because it can lead to unnecessary disputes about how much a tenant feels they should pay this month vs. the previous month. Here's an example of how bill-back could backfire: "I wasn't here half of the month; I shouldn't pay for a whole month," or, "I know tenant A uses the internet way more than I do; they should pay more."

o   Include utility charges in the rent by adding up all charges and dividing them by room or square footage.

# Moving in and Property Management

Now that you have a qualified tenant, it's time to move them into the property. There are a few practices that will help you manage roommate situations effectively and avoid common headaches if you put in the work upfront. The goal is to set the expectation from day one that your property is a clean, functional, inviting and modern living space, and you plan to keep it that way.

## Why You Should Furnish Your Rental Property

- Easy Tenant Turnover
  - Functional furniture gets the most out of common spaces, and tenant turnover becomes effortless because all they need to pack up are their belongings from their room, fridge and bathroom. You can find affordable, functional furniture from Ikea, American Furniture Warehouse, and my personal favorite, Facebook Marketplace. Keep it simple and not too comfortable (no super comfy couch, a big screen TV and Xbox). The last thing you want is several guests in your property partying or lounging around taking over all the common areas.

- Promotes Peaceful Communal Living
  - Providing furniture such as a kitchen table, chairs, bar stools, couches, end tables, etc. makes your new tenant feel right at home, and you won't have to worry about the clutter of extra couches and chairs.

  - Avoid the struggles and confusion of separate kitchen utensils, pots and pans, plates, cups, silverware, etc. by providing basic kitchen necessities.

  - The refrigerator space doesn't have to be confusing to navigate, simply divide the space out by assigning individual shelves for tenant's food. Designate the door as communal space.

## Six Property Management Tips to Save Time (and headaches)

Whether you are managing your own property or having someone else manage it for you, there are a lot of things that need to be decided on to set yourself up for long-term success. This is not an easy process but has rewards that can contribute to building long-term wealth.

- Collecting Rent Payments
  - Always have documented transactions. Accepting payments in cash is ok, but you need a clear paper trail for every payment received. This is ultimately important when you go to qualify for a new loan. The lender will need to see how, when and the amount of collected rent documented.

  - Get the assurance of compliance and security with mobile applications like Venmo, Zelle and PayPal—they will be your new best friends. When you collect rent using Cozy.co, payments will be transferred directly to your bank account, and if you don't receive payment on the day you specify, they'll let your tenant know and automatically add a late fee to encourage payments on-time—no need to knock on doors or have to follow-up.

- Establish Office Hours
  - Set the expectations up front because there isn't much you can do about a clogged toilet at midnight. Choose your availability by setting reasonable office hours to eliminate late-night phone calls for non-emergency issues.

- Managing Landlord-Roommate Relationship
  - People may have less than ideal experiences with landlords, so if they're living in your property, should you tell them you're the owner? It's up to you, but I suggest for you to be honest and up front. Plenty of landlords make it work either way.

- o The advantages of being a live-in-landlord is that you're seen as an authoritative figure, not their friend. Tenants are more likely to refrain from property damage and noise violations, and you'll have the ability to settle disputes quickly. Communication is key. Always refer to the lease when resolving issues.

- ▪ Property Upgrades
  - o One important goal is to get top dollar for your property, so upgrading to meet modern standards is encouraged, but keep in mind, there's a major difference between a House Hack vs. Your Dream Property—a HUGE difference. Don't renovate your rental as if it were your dream home.

  - o Renters want a comfortable, functional, clean and safe place to live. Renters don't care about stainless steel appliances, marble countertops or pricy light fixtures, so don't waste money on luxurious upgrades.

  - o What should you improve to add the most value? Low-key landscaping is important to attract tenants and sets the tone for the inside of the property. Dead grass and overgrown weeds are unappealing. Kitchens are often the focal point of and can improve the value of your property. Upgrading a kitchen can cost anywhere from 5-20k. Remember, tenants don't care about fancy appliances, backsplashes or cabinets. Adding bedrooms/bathrooms increases your rental income because it'll attract more potential tenants, and it boosts the value of your property, making it a great return on investment long-term.

- ▪ Hiring Contractors

- o Generally, contractors are not hard to find. When your property needs repairs outside of your scope of expertise or you don't have time on your hands, I recommend asking for personal recommendations from close friends, other investors and inspectors.

- o Licensed Vs. Non-Licensed: The purpose of contractor licensing is to ultimately reduce liability for homeowners and increase legitimacy of the work, even if they are more expensive. Typically, unlicensed contractors charge less because they avoid worker's compensation and liability insurance requirements.

- o If you choose to do the work yourself, you'll avoid paying for a contractor, but there is an opportunity cost involved since you're sacrificing your free time.

- Self-Manage Vs. Property Manager

  - o Self-managing a property is a large undertaking, but if you have the time on your hands, it yields a higher profit margin since you will not have to spend your earnings on management expenses. Just make sure to include a 10% property management (PM) fee in your numbers—you don't want to self-manage forever.

  - o If you are a full-time employee or work two jobs, you may not have time for routine maintenance, responding to repair requests, lockouts or managing vacancies. It may be worth leaving management duties to an experienced property manager. The goal for every investor should be to have someone else manage their property.

Like most topics we have covered in this course, the process of finding, screening and managing your own tenants is a personal choice that you will have to make. You will need to weigh the pros and cons to determine the best course of action for your individual situation.

Most importantly, make sure you have the dedication to the underwriting process so that you can form productive habits, set good expectations and set yourself up for success long-term.

Jeff is an avid house hacker and helps other investors and house hackers run their properties. He offers coaching sessions to get started, how to run a house hack efficiently and can answer any operation questions. All of our clients receive a complimentary session with Jeff once we close on a house hack property.

If you have more questions about how to run a quality house hack or want to connect with Jeff, please email him at thehousehackingcoach@gmail.com

House hackers who work with Chris and his team to buy an investment property receive a copy of our house hacking lease for free and a complimentary consulting package with Jeff to help with leasing.

# Chapter 13

# Buying Your Next House Hack

In this section, we will be talking about preparing to buy your next house hack property. Whether it's moving from your first house hack to your second or your fifth house hack, we will help you with the steps needed to transition to that next one. We will go through some considerations you will want to keep in mind when planning your next house hack and turning your current house hack into a rental.

## Checklist for next Property:

- **Review strategy and assess current market and portfolio**
  - Take a step back. Look at your current strategy and evaluate the current performance of your property/properties, the market and your finances.
  - Check in with your team (agent, lender, coach) to make sure everyone is still on the same page.
  - Make changes as necessary.
- **Lending**
  - Do you have the down payment and acquisition costs saved?
    - At least 5% + acquisition costs ready to go.

- ○ Can you qualify for the new mortgage with or without a lease and income from your current house hack?

  - ▪ Check with the lender two to four months before you plan to purchase the next property so that you can make sure everything is lined up correctly and there won't be any issues to qualify for the next loan (ex. Is your credit still good? Have you been reporting rents correctly?)

- ○ Occupancy rule timeline compliance.

  - ▪ Have you lived in your property for 12 months to meet the occupancy requirement?

  - ▪ Remember, refinances may reset the 12-month timeline.

- ▪ **Finances**

  - ○ Do you have sufficient liquid reserves for your current properties and the new one?

  - ○ As mentioned in a previous chapter, we recommend six months of PITI or $10,000 per property.

- ▪ **Tenants**

  - ○ What's the plan for your current house hack?

    - ▪ Are you moving out and replacing your spot with one or more renters?

    - ▪ Are you moving everyone out and renting to long-term renters?

  - ○ What's the plan for the new house?

    - ▪ Know when your closing is so you can start marketing.

None of this is rocket science but these are important things to keep in mind. You always want to be thinking ahead so you can know what to expect and plan how you will move forward. It's better to have a plan and have it change than no plan at all.

A unique service that our team provides is an annual review to go over your finances, goals and market changes so we can make any needed adjustments to your strategy and set new goals. Our main objective is to be your long-term real estate investment advisor.

# Chapter 14

# Play the Long Game

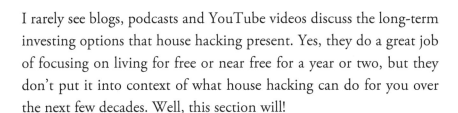

I rarely see blogs, podcasts and YouTube videos discuss the long-term investing options that house hacking present. Yes, they do a great job of focusing on living for free or near free for a year or two, but they don't put it into context of what house hacking can do for you over the next few decades. Well, this section will!

As you're buying multiple house hacks, there are three main themes going on:

## #1: Experience and Knowledge

Gaining experience and knowledge is vital, but it doesn't show up on a spreadsheet or your profit and loss statement! It's very hard to measure, but every deal you buy and every year that you own a property builds your knowledge and experience. We often cite house hacking as a great launching pad. As you accumulate capital and want to move into bigger deals and partnerships, this knowledge becomes invaluable and a powerful resource.

The experience that Joe, Jeff and I have each gained from our investing experience has helped us win deals and make smarter investing decisions. I have represented Jeff on a couple of his house hack purchases where we've run against other offers coming in. Guess what? My team and I "sell" Jeff and his experience as an experienced investor as one who can perform and won't get stuck on minor details during the inspection process. It's helped us win the properties!

As you grow, keep this in the back of your mind. Both during the good times and the bad times. There will be both, and they will make you a better investor.

# #2: Cash Flow

After reviewing a couple of deals, it's obvious that you're not getting rich off the initial cash flow. That's fine and is to be expected. If you're patient and play the long game, your cash flow should increase. What's your biggest expense on a property? It's your monthly mortgage payment. It's a fixed monthly amount. Your payment in month one is the same as month 201. In Denver, rents have grown an average of 4% per year. Can we guarantee that they'll continue to grow? No, we can't, but there's a high probability that they will. Remember, your mortgage payment, assuming a 30-year fixed loan, is inflation proof!

In addition to the cash flow, you'll receive the depreciation tax benefits. They'll put cash flow back into your bank account every year.

# #3: Equity Build

There are two ways you build equity in a property:

1. Appreciation
2. Debt pay down

Is appreciation guaranteed? No, it's not, but it's highly likely. Over the last 45 years, Denver has seen an average appreciation rate of approximately 6%. In the last 44 years in Denver, every year, except for four years, prices have appreciated. Will we see a 6% appreciation growth in the future? I honestly don't know. I do think Denver will continue to appreciate. With all the job and population growth, how can it not? I've asked this question to hundreds of people and to-date not a single person believes Denver will be worth less in the future than it is today. Now, I'm not saying there won't be plateaus or possible down periods, but overall, I'm bullish on Denver and want to ride the wave of growth.

Every time you pay your monthly mortgage, a portion of your payment goes toward principal reduction. As long as you make your payments, you're building equity.

The next page shows the "Long-Term Analysis" tab of Joe's spreadsheet of the room by room house hack Aurora example. Spend a few minutes to really study it. Here are some items to focus on:

- Compare row 31 (Annual Mortgage Payments) to row 29 (Net Operating Income). The annual mortgage payments stay the same! The net operating income shows the money left over after both increased rents and expenses. The spread or profit is increasing!

- Look at row 32 (Annual Mortgage Insurance). It drops off between years 9 and 10. Thus, increasing your cash flow!

- Row 38 (Total Equity) shows the equity from appreciation and debt paydown. Every year it grows quite a bit. We're using a conservative 3% appreciation rate.

- Look at the ROI Quadrant™ returns on rows 41 to 45. Not bad for only 5% down.

Due to limited space, we couldn't show out to year 30. Plus, the text may be hard to read. If you'd like a copy of this spreadsheet, reach out to us and we'd be happy to share it so you can study it in detail.

| | | Year 1 | Year 2 | Year 3 | Year 4 | Year 5 | Year 10 | Year 15 |
|---|---|---|---|---|---|---|---|---|
| 9 | **Annual Income** | | | | | | | |
| 10 | Annual Rental Income | $ 38,400 | $ 39,552 | $ 40,739 | $ 41,961 | $ 43,220 | $ 50,103 | $ 58,083 |
| 11 | Vacancy 5% | $ (1,920) | $ (1,978) | $ (2,037) | $ (2,098) | $ (2,161) | $ (2,505) | $ (2,904) |
| 12 | Expected Annual Rental Income | $ 36,480 | $ 37,574 | $ 38,702 | $ 39,863 | $ 41,059 | $ 47,598 | $ 55,179 |
| 15 | **Annual Expenses** | | | | | | | |
| 16 | Reserves for Repairs and Maintenance | $ 3,072 | $ 3,164 | $ 3,259 | $ 3,357 | $ 3,458 | $ 4,008 | $ 4,547 |
| 18 | Real Estate Taxes | $ 2,224 | $ 2,291 | $ 2,359 | $ 2,430 | $ 2,503 | $ 2,902 | $ 3,364 |
| 19 | Property Insurance | $ 978 | $ 1,007 | $ 1,038 | $ 1,069 | $ 1,101 | $ 1,276 | $ 1,479 |
| 20 | Utilities (if paid by owner) | | | | | | | |
| 21 | - Water and Sewer | $ 1,200 | $ 1,236 | $ 1,273 | $ 1,311 | $ 1,351 | $ 1,566 | $ 1,815 |
| 22 | - Trash | $ 300 | $ 309 | $ 318 | $ 328 | $ 338 | $ 392 | $ 454 |
| 23 | - Electric | $ 1,500 | $ 1,545 | $ 1,591 | $ 1,639 | $ 1,688 | $ 1,957 | $ 2,269 |
| 24 | - Landscaping | $ - | | | | | | |
| 25 | - Internet | $ 500 | $ 618 | $ 637 | $ 656 | $ 675 | $ 783 | $ 908 |
| 26 | - Other | $ - | | | | | | |
| 27 | **Total Annual Expenses** | $ 9,874 | $ 10,170 | $ 10,475 | $ 10,790 | $ 11,113 | $ 12,883 | $ 14,935 |
| 29 | **Net Operating Income** | $ 26,606 | $ 27,404 | $ 28,226 | $ 29,073 | $ 29,945 | $ 34,715 | $ 40,244 |
| 31 | Less: Annual Mortgage Payments | $ (20,103) | $ (20,103) | $ (20,103) | $ (20,103) | $ (20,103) | $ (20,103) | $ (20,103) |
| 32 | Less: Annual Mortgage Insurance | $ (1,532) | $ (1,532) | $ (1,532) | $ (1,532) | $ (1,532) | $ - | $ - |
| 34 | **Annual Cash Flow Before Taxes** | $ 4,971 | $ 7,302 | $ 8,124 | $ 8,970 | $ 9,843 | $ 14,612 | $ 20,141 |
| 36 | Property Value at End of Year | $ 386,250 | $ 397,838 | $ 409,773 | $ 422,066 | $ 434,728 | $ 503,969 | $ 584,738 |
| 37 | Mortgage Balance at End of Year | $ 349,839 | $ 343,175 | $ 336,248 | $ 329,048 | $ 321,564 | $ 279,476 | $ 228,405.96 |
| 38 | **Total Equity** | $ 36,411 | $ 54,662 | $ 73,524 | $ 93,017 | $ 113,163 | $ 224,492 | $ 355,832 |
| 40 | **ROI Quadrant™** | | | | | | | |
| 41 | Appreciation | $11,250 — 42.0% | $11,588 — 43.3% | $11,935 — 44.6% | $12,293 — 45.9% | $12,662 — 47.3% | $14,679 — 54.8% | $17,017 — 63.6% |
| 42 | Cash Flow | $4,971 — 18.6% | $7,302 — 27.3% | $8,124 — 30.4% | $8,970 — 33.5% | $9,843 — 36.8% | $14,612 — 54.6% | $20,141 — 75.3% |
| 43 | Debt Paydown | $6,411 — 24.0% | $6,664 — 24.9% | $6,927 — 25.9% | $7,200 — 26.9% | $7,484 — 28.0% | $9,081 — 33.9% | $11,019 — 41.2% |
| 44 | Cash Flow From Depreciation | $2,898 — 10.8% | $2,898 — 10.8% | $2,898 — 10.8% | $2,898 — 10.8% | $2,898 — 10.8% | $2,898 — 10.8% | $2,898 — 10.8% |
| 45 | **Total Return on Investment** | $25,530 — 95.4% | $28,451 — 106.3% | $29,883 — 111.7% | $31,361 — 117.2% | $32,886 — 122.9% | $41,270 — 154.2% | $51,075 — 190.8% |

See All Years

# Different Scenarios for Achieving $10,000/mo.

Let's continue with the common goal of achieving $10,000/mo. in rental income. Remember, you'll need approximately $15,000 in gross rents from properties with **no mortgages**. Using the same Aurora house hack example, you would need six houses bringing in a long-term rental income of $2,500/mo. (6 * $2,500 = $15,000). For long-term modeling, I revert back to traditional rentals. Self-managing six rentals with room by room rentals is not a hands-off retirement. The simplest plan is to house hack six times and then use the debt snowball method to pay them off.

Is it possible? Absolutely. It's the most straightforward and simple plan. However, very few investors will house hack six times. Many people get fatigued or life changes after three or four properties. It's a great initial plan to start with because everyone needs a simple plan to start working towards. It's not worth stressing about the details of property #6 when you're still on property #1.

The rest of this chapter will discuss three strategies that you can use to accelerate you towards your goal. They are:

- A rate and term refinance to increase cash flow.
- A cash out refinance to buy more properties.
- A 1031 exchange transaction to buy more rental properties.

Is one better than the other? Nope. There are a lot of factors as to which, if any, you should do. They are all options that are available after owning a property, typically for at least a few years. Let's run through some examples.

# Rate and Term Refinance to Increase Cash Flow

A rate and term refinance is when you refinance the loan on your property to change the interest rate and, possibly, the term of the loan. Investors typically do this if interest rates are lower than when they purchased the property and/or to drop mortgage insurance.

At the time of publishing this guide, Jeff just finished doing a rate and term refinance on his fourplex house hack with Joe. He purchased the fourplex with an FHA loan to utilize the favorable low down payment option that it provided. However, he had mortgage insurance of $400/mo. for the life of the loan. Since purchasing the property, two things have happened:

1. Interest rates have dropped.
2. He has enough equity of 25% to do an investment refinance loan.

The table below compares not only the loan differences, but also the equity and rent differences as well. It's a great example of what happens when you have patience with real estate:

| | 2017 FHA Loan | 2020 Conventional Loan | Difference |
|---|---|---|---|
| Interest Rate | 3.75% | 3.625% | 0.125% |
| Payment (Principal and Interest) | $2,754.28 | $2,656.58 | $97.70 |

| Mortgage Insurance | $400 | $0 | $400 |
|---|---|---|---|
| Property Value | $630,000 | $815,000 | $185,000 |
| Rents | $3,785 | $4775 | $990 |

In Jeff's case, interest rates dropped. Even if rates didn't drop, refinancing would still make sense (as long as rates didn't increase too much) to drop the monthly mortgage insurance of $400/mo. Between dropping mortgage insurance of $400 and reducing his monthly payment by $97, his monthly cash flow increased by almost $500/mo. That's a significant increase in cash flow!

It costs money to refinance a loan. Since Jeff has a significant equity increase, he paid zero out-of-pocket to refinance. Joe was able to wrap the refinance costs into the new loan.

In addition to saving money with the refinance, rents also increased by $990/mo. Between the increased rents of $990 and monthly savings of $497, his cash flow has increased by $1,487 since purchasing the property.

This is a great example of what happens when you're a smart investor and play the long game.

The one downside is that Jeff's FHA loan had 27 years left on it. The new loan has 30 years left on it. An extra three years to save $500/mo. is a smart trade off.

Here's a key point: regardless of whether Jeff refinanced or not, once the loan is paid off, the property will perform the same and generate the same cash flow. The difference now is that he can use the extra $500/mo. to save towards buying additional properties.

# Cash-Out Refinance

A cash-out refinance is when you refinance the loan to take cash out. Don't expect to buy a property at 5% down and do a cash-out refi the following year. That is highly unlikely. It often takes three to seven years to build enough equity in order to take cash out because you still need to leave 25% equity in the property for an investment loan. Let's discuss two examples of taking cash out for investing purposes.

# Example #1: Cash-Out to Buy Future Nomads™

In 2019, one of my clients wanted to start Nomading™ to build a rental portfolio. The clients have two young kids, so house hacking with roommates was not a good fit for their family. They wanted to start acquiring properties.

Years ago, before they became interested in real estate investing, they purchased a house. We sat down to discuss options with the current house. The house made sense to keep as a rental property. Like many Denver homeowners, they were sitting on a significant chunk of equity. During our investment strategy meeting, we realized that tapping into the equity would allow them to buy Nomad™ properties quicker than if they relied on their savings rate alone.

We had Joe run two different scenarios for doing a cash-out refinance:

1. An owner-occupant refinance. Just like when they purchased, these have lower interest rates and have a one-year requirement to live there. **Yes, even though they've already lived there, if they did this option, they are required to live there for one year from the date of the new loan's closing.**

2. An investment cash-out refinance. These come with a higher interest rate but have no occupancy requirement. They can move out at any time.

The table below compares the two options:

|  | Owner Occupant Cash-Out Refi | Investment Cash-Out Refi | Difference |
|---|---|---|---|
| Interest Rate | 3.5% | 3.875% | 0.375% |
| Payment (Principal and Interest) | 1,549 | $1,622 | $73 |
| Mortgage Insurance | $0 | $0 | --- |
| Cash-Out Amount | $88,700 | $82,042 | $6,658 |

The important question we wanted answered was, "Is the owner-occupant refi savings worth staying there another year?" As you can see above, they would save $73/mo. and get an extra $6,685 cash-out at closing. They get more cash with the owner-occupant refinance because there were less points for them to buy down. For both options they were using the equity in their home to pay for all the closing costs and point buy down.

Before we answer the question, it's important to understand more about their personal situation. They have two young boys who start kindergarten in three years. Once they start school, they'll most likely stop Nomading™ so the kids can stay in the same school. Their goal is to acquire a few rental properties before settling down within a school district.

The monthly savings of $73/mo. and an extra $6,685 in cash was not worth it to them to stay there another year. I agree with their decision. They decided to go with the investment cash-out refinance loan option and bought their next property in Q1 2020.

They are disciplined clients who took the cash-out refinance to help fund the down payments on their future properties. The cash from their first place is going to help them buy three more properties!

# Example #2: Cash-Out Refinance to Buy Rental

In November 2019, I closed on a cash-out refinance on my primary residence to pull out $106,000 to invest into Denver rental properties. In this example, the construction we did on the house forced appreciation. It normally takes about 3-7 years for a house hack to create the market appreciation needed, but the concept here still applies.

The new loan increased my monthly mortgage payment by $480. This chapter will walk you through all the details of my decision-making process to pull the trigger and why I'm happy to spend $480/mo. to have $106,000 to invest now.

# Determining the Amount of Equity

My wife and I are house hacking by having her mother live with us to help reduce living expenses, namely daycare for our little ones. All of us wanted separate living spaces. Unfortunately, we couldn't find a home that met our needs with an existing mother-in-law suite. Instead, we bought a home with a walkout basement.

In 2018, we remodeled the basement into a beautiful mother-in-law suite. The original budget was $75,000, but it ended up totaling about $100,000. Damn scope creep! Well, it was expected. The budget always goes up on remodels. The basement is about 1,400 square feet and now has a full kitchen, living room, master bedroom, master bath and a guest bedroom. The finishes are quite a few steps above rental grade finishes.

Spending $100,000 to remodel a basement is a lot of money, but it's a complete win/win from a personal and financial perspective. From the financial perspective, my MIL didn't want a monthly mortgage payment, and we didn't want to outlay a huge chunk of cash. My MIL sold her previous home, used some of the proceeds to fund the remodel, and we will take care of all the on-going costs and the mortgage.

Estimating the new value was very hard to do because there are no good comps. Typically, one can pull some comps to get a quick ballpark or have an agent run a CMA (Comparative Market Analysis). There were no great comparable properties that I could find on the MLS.

---

*During a cash-out refinance, who determines the value of the property? It's not me, you or the market. It's the appraiser.*

---

Spending $100,000 in upgrades does not directly translate into a $100,000 value increase. Generally speaking, the total amount spent on upgrades will NOT increase your home's value by the same amount. Home upgrades typically give you a very poor ROI. Even if I got 50 cents on the dollar, I could still pull out some money to invest between the upgrades and some market appreciation.

I called up Joe Massey at Castle & Cooke Mortgage to start the cash-out refinance paperwork. It's $600 for an appraisal. Worst case scenario, I'd be out $600 if it didn't come in at a value of $700,000 or higher to make it worthwhile for a cash-out refinance. I started the paperwork and paid for the appraisal.

## The Appraisal

Since I'm an agent, I see more appraisals than the average investor. Here's the interesting thing—you can have three different appraisers appraise the same property and get back three different values, and all three are correct! The appraiser is giving his or her expert *opinion* based on their knowledge and available data. Appraisers determine the value by talking with agents who sold properties they are using as comps, using information that they have compiled over the years and using data on the property from the MLS.

I scheduled the appraisal for when I was home to walk the property and answer his questions. Before the appraiser came over, I made copies of all the receipts, work orders, budget plans and anything else related to the basement remodel. My goal was to provide him with as much data as possible so he could accurately value my house.

We spent 45 minutes walking the property, discussing the upgrades and answering his questions. If you've never met with an appraiser or read a report, it's nothing exciting, but it was 45 minutes well spent.

He left, and the appraisal came back a few days later...

---

*It appraised at $775,000!*

---

It was above my $700,000 threshold to make the cash-out refi worth it. YES!

# Reviewing the Cash-Out Refinance Options

I'm not a lender nor an expert on cash-out refinances. Make sure you talk with a lender to get details specific to your situation as there are many different options available.

My existing mortgage balance was approximately $430,000. The new cash-out refinance has to pay off the existing mortgage amount. The difference (minus closing costs) is the cash that I get to take out.

## Consideration #1: Loan to Value (LTV)

I'm a fan of maximizing leverage while holding high cash reserves to minimize risk. The same concept applies to the cash-out refinance on my primary.

A 75% LTV is typically the sweet spot for maximizing a cash-out refi, while also getting the best interest rates. Since it's my primary, an 80% LTV option was available, but it came with a higher interest rate. **The higher interest rate was NOT worth the trade-off for pulling out a few more dollars.**

75% of $775,000 = $581,250. The 2019 conforming loan limit for Douglas County is $561,200. If I did a 75% LTV, then my loan would fall under a "high balance loan." I don't know the details of it other than it has a higher interest rate. The extra $20,000 that I could pull out was not worth the higher interest rate.

---

*For my situation, it made the most sense to maximize to the conforming loan value of $561,200 or a 72.4% LTV.*

---

# Consideration #2: Buying Down the Interest Rate

Joe presented me with four different interest rate options. The original interest rate required no discount points. The lower the rate goes, the more money I have to pay upfront to buy the interest rate down. Below is a table that breaks everything down. Descriptions of each row are below the table.

| Interest Rate | 5.125% | 4.75% | 4.125% | 3.75% |
|---|---|---|---|---|
| Loan Amount | $561,200 | $561,200 | $561,200 | $561,200 |
| Closing Costs | $3,122 | $3,122 | $3,122 | $3,122 |
| Escrow (taxes, insurance) | $3,222 | $3,222 | $3,222 | $3,222 |
| Discount Points | 0 | 0.750% $4,209 | 1.750% $9,821 | 2.5% $14,030 |
| Cash-Out | $124,214 | $120,017 | $114,424 | $110,227 |
| Monthly P&I | $3,055 | $2,927 | $2,719 | $2,599 |
| Break-even period (months) | 0 | 33 | 29 | 31 |

**Interest rate** - This is the final note rate for the 30-year loan.

**Loan amount** - It stays the same at $561,200, which is the maximum amount for Douglas County, CO in 2019.

**Closing costs** - It stays the same at $3,122. Here's a breakdown:

- Processing fee: $745
- Underwriting fee: $795
- Discount points are included but have a separate row (see below.)
- Appraisal fee: $600 (I paid this directly and outside of the closing table)
- Title - Settlement fee: $240
- Title - Lender's title insurance policy: $1,175
- Mortgage recording fee: $167

**Discount points** - The amount I'm paying to buy the rate down. 1 point equals 1 percent of the total loan amount. For example, take the discount point of 0.75% x $561,200 = $4,209. The row shows the percent and the dollar figure.

**Cash-out** - The total amount of cash I walk away with.

**Monthly P&I (Principal and Interest)** - My monthly mortgage amount before taxes and insurance.

**Break-even period (months)** - How many months will it take for me to break even between the amount spent on the point buydown and the monthly savings? The monthly mortgage payment savings on the 3.75% loan vs. the 5.125% loan is $456 ($3,055 - $2,599). Simply divide the discount points paid by the monthly savings to determine how many months it takes to break even: $14,030 / $456 = 31 months, or about 2.5 years.

---

*I chose the 3.75% rate option with the $14,030 point buy down.*

---

I spent a couple days debating which option to go with. Ultimately, the 3.75% option won out for me. Here's why:

- From a personal budgeting perspective, I wanted to keep my PITI (principal, interest, taxes, insurance) around $3,000/mo.

- The $14,000 cash-out difference doesn't move the needle on buying more rentals—getting $100k+ does.

- My original mortgage payment is $2,118/mo. for PI. The 3.75% option "costs" me an extra $480/mo. to get $110,000. The 5.125% option would "cost" me $937/mo. for $124,000.

Spending twice as much each month for an extra $14,000 wasn't worth it to me.

The above table shows the estimated cash-out refinance numbers. After all the documents were signed, I walked away with $106,500 for my cash-out refinance. Why the $4,000 difference?

- The original estimates assumed a closing at the end of the month. We ended up closing early the following month, which had a much higher amount for prepaid interest (28 days vs. 2 days).
- The actual loan payoff for my existing mortgage was higher than in the estimates.

# Investing the Cash

Some investors will only do a cash-out refinance if the new rental property's cash flow is equal to or greater than the difference in their new mortgage payment. I would like to see the cash flow be greater, but it's not a hard and fast rule for me since rental cash flow is not everything.

I will NOT be using the cash flow from the rental property to pay the difference in my new, higher mortgage. One of my current investing rules is to keep my personal finances and investment income completely separate. My budget allows for the extra $480/mo. in my mortgage payment. I look at it as a small loan where I'll happily pay $480/mo. to access $106,000 right now for investing.

Going beyond cash flow and optimizing return on equity will give me a far greater return over the next 30 years. If I can keep the $106,500 amount growing at 10%+ a year, I'll be very happy with those returns. Using the power of leverage and repositioning equity, I'm confident that I can.

# 3/2 Aurora Condo Investment Example

I'll reference the 3/2 condos in Aurora that we purchase regularly for modeling purposes. For the sake of simplicity, I plugged them in as one property into the rental property analyzer spreadsheet. I doubled the expenses and rents as appropriate. It may be off by a few dollars, but it's close enough.

| Property Address | Two condos |
|---|---|
| Number of Units | 2 |

| | |
|---|---|
| Down Payment Percentage | 25% |

| | | |
|---|---|---|
| Purchase Price | $ | 400,000 |
| Acquisition Costs | $ | 10,000 |
| Loan Costs | $ | 1,540 |
| Down Payment | $ | 100,000 |
| Mortgage Balance | $ | 300,000 |
| Initial Repair Costs | $ | - |
| Total Initial Investment | $ | 111,540 |

| | |
|---|---|
| Mortgage Interest Rate | 4.500% |
| Mortgage Term (years) | 30 |

### MONTHLY Rental Income Per Unit

| | | |
|---|---|---|
| Unit #1 | $ | 1,850 |
| Unit #2 | $ | 1,850 |
| Unit #3 | $ | - |
| Unit #4 | $ | - |
| Total Rental Income | $ | 3,700 |

| | |
|---|---|
| Vacancy Factor | 5% |
| Annual Appreciation Rate | 3% |
| Effective Tax Rate | 25% |

## Monthly Operating Expenses

| | |
|---|---|
| Do you pay for property management? | Yes |
| Monthly Cost for Property Management - Percentage | 8% |
| Monthly Reserves for Maintenance - Percentage | 5.0% |
| Is there an HOA | Yes |
| Monthly HOA Dues | $ 598 |

## Additional Annual Expenses

| | |
|---|---|
| Annual Real Estate Taxes | $ 2,100 |
| Annual Property Insurance | $ 700 |
| Utilities (If paid by owner) | |
| - Water and Sewer | $ - |
| - Trash | $ - |
| - Electric | $ - |
| Landscaping | $ - |

The total initial investment needed will probably be $111,000, possibly a few thousand dollars more if any initial repairs are needed. The difference of $5,000 between my cash-out refi is something that I can make up.

# 1st Year Returns

- Cash-on-cash return: 7.3%
- Cap rate: 6.6%

# Return on Investment Quadrant™

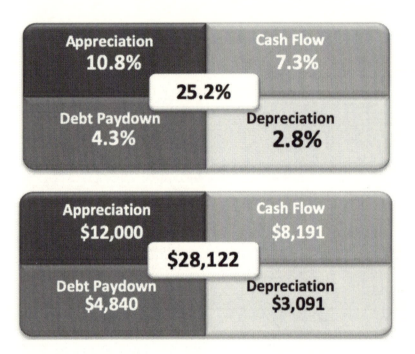

Cash flow comparison:

- My higher mortgage is +$480/mo. or $5,760/yr.
- The cash flow from the two condos is $8,191/yr.

---

*The rental property's cashflow is $2,431 more than my increased mortgage payment. Win!*

*It's an estimated 25% ROI on my money. Win, Win!*

*Don't forget about depreciation at $3,091/yr. Another win!*

---

Don't forget about depreciation. That should bring in another $3,091 a year in cash flow come tax time. Think about this: the depreciation benefits alone cover more than 50% of my higher mortgage payment.

## The Big Picture (and Big Win!)

Too many people get hyper focused on the cash flow difference between the rental property and their new mortgage payment in the first year or two. Go beyond cash flow and beyond a few years to evaluate the big picture.

---

*In 10 years, the two condos should return:*

*$81,910 in cumulative cash flow (assuming no rent increases) and $297,000 in equity.*

---

The new mortgage payment difference will cost me $57,600 ($480 * 12 months * 10 years). Remember, this is a 30-year fixed mortgage, so my payment amount does NOT go up.

Is spending $57,600 to make almost $400,000 a good investment? Yes!

Assuming you take all your rental profit and simply save it in a bank account, you should have enough to buy one more rental.

What's the equity opportunity cost on $297,000? A lot depends on how good these are as rentals in 10 years. Perhaps the complex shifts from investors to owner-occupant and it's time to cash-out. Who knows? With that much equity, you'll have options to refinance or sell to buy more rental properties.

Remember, this is 10 years out on the 30-year refinance loan. What's the return look like over 30 years saving cash flow and maximizing equity opportunity costs a few times by selling or refinancing? It looks pretty good to me.

# Terms Only Refinance

About six months after I did this cash-out refinance, interest rates took a nosedive due to the COVID-19 pandemic. I did a rate and term refinance to lower my interest rate again. My new interest rate is at 2.875%, and my new PI payment is $2,385/mo. It's only $266 more than my original payment. Since this refinance happened in 2020, the loan limits increased from 2019. I didn't do the max 75% LTV cash-out refinance. I was able to refinance again with almost no money out-of-pocket. All I had to pay for was a drive-by appraisal of $350 since the other appraisal happened within one year.

This is a great example of how you can't predict the market and how you can layer these strategies on top of one another.

Now that we have looked at a few examples, it's important to talk about our return on equity.

# Return on Equity

After owning a property for a few years, is using return on initial investment the best way to measure the performance of your rental property? No, it's not. You're building equity, which has an opportunity cost. Do you leave it in the current property or take some or all of it out to buy more properties? What you do or don't do with the equity can have a big impact on your rental portfolio.

This section covers:

- How to calculate and understand return on equity.
- The three common scenarios for determining your equity opportunity costs.
- An overview of the "Equity Optimization" Spreadsheet.
- A real-world case study for optimizing return on equity.

# Return on Investment (ROI) vs. Return on Equity (ROE)

Calculating the return on your initial investment is a great way to analyze rental properties at the time of purchase. After a few years, it becomes an inadequate way to measure your return.

Calculating the ROI is nothing more than a simple fraction that takes your total return and divides it by your total initial investment.

$$\text{Return on Investment (ROI)} = \frac{\text{Cash Flow + Appreciation + Debt Paydown + Depreciation}}{\text{Total Initial Investment (Down Payment + Loan + Acquisition + Rent Ready Costs)}}$$

What happens to the fraction and the math over time? The denominator ("Total Initial Investment") stays the same every year. If your initial investment in a rental property was $50,000 in 2015, it stays at $50,000 every year. The numerator (four returns from real estate) changes every year.

Fast forward to five years after you purchase an investment, calculate your ROI. At year five, you're taking returns in today's dollars and dividing it by an investment from five years ago. The result is not a great way to measure your return. However, return on equity (ROE) is.

Return on equity is taking the four returns of real estate (the numerator) and dividing it by your equity (the denominator):

$$\text{Return on Equity (ROE)} = \frac{\text{Cash Flow + Appreciation + Debt Paydown + Depreciation}}{\text{Equity}}$$

ROE gives you a more accurate return because it's taking numbers from the current year for both the numerator and denominator. Every year, the numerator and denominator are changing.

I put together a table to show you ROE vs. ROI. **The Return on Equity** column takes the four returns and divides it by the current equity in the property. **The Return on Investment** column takes the four returns and divides it by your initial total investment.

Spend a few minutes to review the table but pay particular attention to the **Return on Equity** and **Return on Investment** columns and what happens to their percent returns every year. FYI, the table uses a real-world rental property that is a 3-bedroom, 2-bathroom condo in Aurora. I rounded the purchase up a couple thousand to $200,000 for simplicity.

# Return on Equity Tables

| ROI vs ROE | | | | | |
|---|---|---|---|---|---|
| Year | Return on Equity | Return on Investment | Total Return | Equity | Initial Investment |
| | = Total Return / Equity | = Total Return / Initial Investment | = Cash Flow + Appreciation + Debt Paydown + Depreciation | = down payment + Appreciation + Debt Paydown (Principal Reduction) | = down payment + acquisition + loan + rent ready costs |
| 1 | 32% | 29% | 15,854 | 50,000 | 55,000 |
| 2 | 28% | 30% | 16,591 | 58,459 | 55,000 |
| 3 | 26% | 32% | 17,352 | 67,208 | 55,000 |
| 4 | 24% | 33% | 18,137 | 76,259 | 55,000 |
| 5 | 22% | 34% | 18,947 | 85,621 | 55,000 |
| 6 | 21% | 36% | 19,784 | 95,306 | 55,000 |
| 7 | 20% | 38% | 20,648 | 105,325 | 55,000 |

| 8 | 19% | 39% | 21,540 | 115,692 | 55,000 |
|---|---|---|---|---|---|
| 9 | 18% | 41% | 22,460 | 126,417 | 55,000 |
| 10 | 17% | 43% | 23,411 | 137,514 | 55,000 |
| 11 | 16% | 44% | 24,393 | 148,997 | 55,000 |
| 12 | 16% | 46% | 25,406 | 160,879 | 55,000 |
| 13 | 15% | 48% | 26,452 | 173,174 | 55,000 |
| 14 | 15% | 50% | 27,533 | 185,898 | 55,000 |
| 15 | 14% | 52% | 28,649 | 199,067 | 55,000 |
| 16 | 14% | 54% | 29,801 | 212,696 | 55,000 |
| 17 | 14% | 56% | 30,990 | 226,802 | 55,000 |
| 18 | 13% | 59% | 32,219 | 241,403 | 55,000 |
| 19 | 13% | 61% | 33,488 | 256,516 | 55,000 |
| 20 | 13% | 63% | 34,798 | 272,161 | 55,000 |
| 21 | 13% | 66% | 36,152 | 288,356 | 55,000 |
| 22 | 12% | 68% | 37,550 | 305,123 | 55,000 |
| 23 | 12% | 71% | 38,994 | 322,481 | 55,000 |
| 24 | 12% | 74% | 40,485 | 340,453 | 55,000 |
| 25 | 12% | 76% | 42,025 | 359,061 | 55,000 |
| 26 | 12% | 79% | 43,616 | 378,329 | 55,000 |
| 27 | 11% | 82% | 45,260 | 398,282 | 55,000 |
| 28 | 11% | 83% | 45,413 | 418,943 | 55,000 |
| 29 | 11% | 86% | 47,167 | 440,341 | 55,000 |
| 30 | 11% | 89% | 48,979 | 462,501 | 55,000 |
| 31 | 10% | 92% | 50,667 | 485,452 | 55,000 |
| 32 | 10% | 95% | 52,187 | 500,016 | 55,000 |
| 33 | 10% | 98% | 53,752 | 515,017 | 55,000 |

| 34 | 10% | 101% | 55,365 | 530,467 | 55,000 |
| 35 | 10% | 104% | 57,026 | 546,381 | 55,000 |

*What jumps out to you? The ROE goes DOWN every year while the ROI goes up! Surprising? It surprised me the first time I learned about ROE.*

Appreciation and rent growth are at 3%. The higher the appreciation rate, the faster the equity grows, and the quicker your return goes down.

**It's common to have greater cash flow (more cash in your pocket at the end of the year) but have a lower ROE percentage.** Typically, mortgage payments are fixed and stay the same, which is your biggest expense. Generally, rent increases every year. You're getting a bigger spread (profit) between rental income and expenses.

While you're making more cash flow, your equity is growing, driving your return on equity down.

Is this bad? No, it's just an observation. It ultimately depends on what your goals are and what phase you're in of building your rental portfolio.

## Equity Opportunity Costs

It took me a few months to really wrap my head around the idea of equity opportunity costs. In discussing this with my clients, I've found that many of them had the same learning curve. Here's my best attempt at explaining it in a single chapter.

Envision a real piggy bank. It has a slot on the back to stick loose change in. You can keep putting money into it, but it's not making you any money. Most people eventually open up the piggy bank to use the money. When I was a kid, I used it to buy He Man and Teenage Mutant Ninja Turtle toys. Now, as an adult, I use it to buy assets.

I look at equity as money in my "real estate piggy bank." Your piggy bank grows from market appreciation and your tenants paying down your loan. Once you have enough equity built up, you have the option to open up your piggy bank and tap into your equity. The question is: should you?

That's the opportunity cost! If you tap into your equity, it'll change the performance of your current rental property. My intent is not to convince you to tap into it or not but discuss the pros and cons so you can make the best decision for your real estate goals.

You have three options with a rental property:

1. Keep it as-is and do nothing. Let the cash flow grow and the equity build.
2. Do a cash-out refinance or get a HELOC to tap into the equity. You retain ownership and can use the equity for other investments.
3. Sell the property to buy other rental properties.

What's the best option? It depends on you, the property and the market.

# Case Study: Optimizing ROE

This is where the discussion gets fun. I'll explain the three options above by sharing my thought process and numbers on a recent personal transaction.

In 2011, before I was an agent or in real estate investing, I bought my very first property. Without knowing it, I was Nomading™ because, after a couple years, I moved out and converted it into a rental. It was a 2-bedroom/2-bathroom condo in Reno, NV purchased for $67,000.

From 2011 to 2019, the rent increased by 30% from $1,000/mo. to $1,300/mo., and the value increased by 235% to around $225,000 from $67,000. **The market gifted me with equity.**

# ROE Option #1: Keep It

I built a spreadsheet called "Equity Opportunity Costs" to run scenarios on properties through these three different options. **The spreadsheet is not available for download. It may be in the future, but for now, I use it for myself and with clients.**

When you're analyzing a rental property, use the current numbers, not what you bought it for years ago. Using today's numbers is key in giving you a correct analysis. **I entered the numbers as if I were buying it as a rental today.**

| OPTION #1: KEEP IT | | |
|---|---|---|
| Property Address | Reno, NV | |
| Value (today) | $229,000 | |
| Loan balance | $36,300 | |
| Equity | $192,700 | |
| | | |
| Annaul Rent ($1,300/mo) | $15,600 | |
| **Operating Expenses (annual)** | | |
| Vacancy | (780) | 5.0% |
| Taxes | (900) | |
| Insurance | (325) | |
| Property Management | (1,560) | 10.0% |
| HOA ($255/mo) | (3,060) | |
| Repairs Reserves | (780) | 5% |
| **TOTAL OpEx** | (7,405) | |
| | | |
| Net Operating Income (NOI) | 8,195 | |
| | | |
| Annual Mortgage Payments | (6,358) | |
| | | |
| **RETURNS** | | |
| Cash Flow | $1,837 | |
| Apprieciation | $6,870 | 3% |
| Debt Paydown | $4,117 | |
| Depreciation | $517 | |
| **TOTAL Return, Current year** | $13,341 | |
| | | |
| **RETURN ON EQUITY** | **6.92%** | |
| | | |
| Cap rate (current) | 3.58% | |

# Option #1: Keep It

Ignore the light grey fields as they are indicators to me for input fields. Here's the analysis:

- It's a 3.58% cap rate if purchased today. Fortunately, I can easily find much better cap rates in Denver.

- I'm making $1,837/year in cash flow. That has a very minimal impact on my lifestyle and savings rate.

- I'm getting a 6.92% return on equity ($13,341 / $192,700.) A 6.9% return doesn't excite me nor is it what I need to achieve my goals. I need more.

All three of these bullet points indicate that I should do something better with the $192,700 in equity than leaving it in the property.

Now, here's the really interesting thing: **I'm getting an almost infinite return on my initial investment on this property!** I purchased the property on a 15-year mortgage with 0% down, and all the closing costs were wrapped into the loan. **I brought zero dollars to the closing table!** It was a private loan. Back then, I knew it was a good deal, but now I realize how amazing the loan was. I really wish I had picked up a few more properties. Oh well.

It's an infinite return because you can't divide by zero. If I plug in the first month's mortgage payment, it came out to a crazy return of around 48,000% over the last 9 years. Yes, that is a forty-eight thousand percent return. Now I'm getting a 6.9% return on my equity. Pretty interesting, huh?

# ROE Option #2A: Max Cash-Out Refinance

Both a HELOC and a cash-out refinance will pull equity out of a property. HELOCs are great if you're going to pay the money back within a one to two-year time frame for flips or BRRRR properties. Cash-out refinances are the ideal choice if you're not paying the money back quickly. The equity would be used as a down payment on another rental, which is a slow payback. I explored doing a cash-out refinance.

**The spreadsheet may be confusing. Read the notes below to understand it.**

| OPTION #2A: Max CASH-OUT REFINANCE | | |
|---|---|---|
| Loan to Value | 75% | |
| Interest Rate | 4.75% | |
| Term (Years) | 30 | |
| New Loan Amount | 171,750 | |
| Less Existing Loan | (36,300) | |
| Refinancing closing costs (2% of loan) | (3,435) | |
| Cash out | 132,015 | |
| New Monthly Payment | 886 | |
| | | |
| **CURRENT PROPERTY PERFORMACE** | | |
| Rent (Annual) | 15,600 | |
| - Operating Expenses | (7,405) | |
| | | |
| Net Operating Income (NOI) | 8,195 | |
| | | |
| - NEW Annual Mortgage Payments | (10,627) | |
| | | |
| **RETURNS** | | Debt Coverage Ratio |
| Cash Flow | (2,432) | 77% |
| Apprieciation | 6,870 | *Stays the same |
| Debt Paydown | 2,698 | |
| Depreciation | 517 | *Stays the same |
| **TOTAL Return, Current year** | 7,653 | |
| | | |
| **RETURN ON EQUITY** | **13.37%** | |

## Option #2A: Max Cash-Out Refinance

**It's a negative cash-flowing property** when doing a max cash-out refinance at a 75% loan-to-value (LTV) loan. Yes, I can pull out $132,000, but the property is negative cash flowing $3,200 a year. **It's a bad idea. It's risky to pull out money and turn your rental into a negative cash-flowing property.**

There is a box labeled "Debt Coverage Ratio" (DCR). I put this calculation in there to measure the risk of how much I should refinance. DCR is a commercial lending underwriting guideline. The formula is DCR = NOI / Annual Debt Service.

The common rule of thumb for lenders is that they want $1.25 in NOI (income after your operating expenses) for every $1 of debt service (just principal and interest). The 25-cent difference is a buffer that they are comfortable with because the property has enough income to pay back their loan.

If you don't understand DCR, don't get hung up on it. Understand that it's a quick way to measure the property performance in terms of the debt load to see if it's "safe" to pull out equity.

# ROE Option #2B: Safe Cash-Out Refinance

Since pulling out the maximum amount of cash is a bad idea, let's pull out a safer and smaller amount of cash.

| OPTION #2B: SAFE CASH-OUT REFINANCE | | |
|---|---|---|
| Loan to Value | 46% | |
| Interest Rate | 4.75% | |
| Term (Years) | 30 | |
| New Loan Amount | 105,340 | |
| Less Existing Loan | (36,300) | |
| Refinancing closing costs (2% of loan) | (2,107) | |
| Cash out | 66,933 | |
| New Monthly Payment | 543 | |
| | | |
| **CURRENT PROPERTY PERFORMACE** | | |
| Rent (Annual) | 15,600 | |
| - Operating Expenses | (7,405) | |
| | | |
| Net Operating Income (NOI) | 8,195 | |
| | | |
| - NEW Annual Mortgage Payments | (6,518) | |
| | | |
| **RETURNS** | | Debt Coverage Ratio |
| Cash Flow | 1,677 | 126% |
| Apprieciation | 6,870 | *Stays the same |
| Debt Paydown | 1,655 | |
| Depreciation | 517 | *Stays the same |
| **TOTAL Return, Current year** | 10,719 | |

## RETURN ON EQUITY    8.67%

## Option #2B: Safe Cash-Out Refinance

**It's a positive cash flowing property with a safe DCR!** However, I'm making about $1,677/yr. in cash flow and will have $66,933 in cash. **However, it's a 46% LTV loan.** I wouldn't put 59% down as a down payment, so does it make sense to leave that much equity in there? Not for me since I'm currently in my accumulation phase of buying rentals, but it's a safe option to pull out equity. Let's compare it to option #3.

# ROE Option #3: Sell to Buy Better Rentals

This is the simplest part of the spreadsheet.

| OPTION #3: SELL IT | |
| --- | --- |
| Sales Price | 229,000 |
| Loan pay off | (36,300) |
| Selling costs | (18,700) |
| | |
| Cash Proceeds | 174,000 |

I'm selling an asset and losing the returns that it generates, but I'm walking away with $174,000 to use to buy other rentals.

It's important to note that doing a cash-out refi is NOT a taxable event. Selling your property is a taxable event. Many investors who sell utilize a 1031 exchange to defer their capital gains taxes.

# Comparing the Three Options

I built a summary page on the spreadsheet to compare the three options. The majority of it is restating what was covered above. It's designed to give a high-level overview of returns from each scenario. To help explain it, screenshots for each section are below with commentary.

The **"New Rental Assumptions Inputs"** section is where to enter the rental property data. It's not analyzing a specific property, but rather taking the current market and interest data to calculate ballpark returns.

| NEW RENTAL ASSUMPTION INPUTS | | | |
|---|---|---|---|
| Market cap rate | 6.00% | Appreciation Rate | 3% |
| Down Payment Percentage | 25% | Tax Bracket | 25% |
| Interest Rate | 4.75% | % Improved | 85% |
| Term (Years) | 30 | | |

## "New Rental Assumptions Inputs" Section

The **"Current Rental"** section is pulling data from the previous tabs of the existing rental and displaying the returns from each scenario.

| | #1: Keep It | #2A: Max Refi | #2B: Safe Refi | #3: Sell it |
|---|---|---|---|---|
| **Current Rental** | | | | |
| Cash Flow | 1,837 | (2,432) | 1,677 | 0 |
| Apprieciation | 6,870 | 6,870 | 6,870 | 0 |
| Debt Paydown | 4,117 | 2,698 | 1,655 | 0 |
| Depreciation | 517 | 517 | 517 | 0 |
| **Total current return:** | 13,341 | 7,653 | 10,719 | 0 |
| | | | | |
| Return on Equity | 6.9% | 13.4% | 8.7% | 0 |
| | | | | |
| Cash from equity | 0 | 132,015 | 66,933 | 174,000 |

The "cash from equity" becomes the downpayment on the new rental property

## "Current Rental" Section

The **"New Rental"** section takes the equity pulled out from the current rental "Cash from equity" row to use it as a down payment on purchasing a new rental using the data from "New Rental Assumption Inputs." It then calculates the returns on the new rental property.

| | #1: Keep It | #2A: Max Refi | #2B: Safe Refi | #3: Sell it |
|---|---|---|---|---|
| **New Rental** | | | | |
| Purchase price | 0 | 528,060 | 267,733 | 696,000 |
| Net Operating Income (NOI) | 0 | 31,684 | 16,064 | 41,760 |
| Debt service (annual) | 0 | (24,505) | (12,424) | (32,298) |
| | | | | |
| **New Rental Returns:** | | | | |
| Cash Flow | 0 | 7,179 | 3,640 | 9,462 |
| Appreciation | 0 | 15,842 | 8,032 | 20,880 |
| Debt Paydown | 0 | 6,222 | 3,154 | 8,200 |
| Depreciation | 0 | 4,080 | 2,069 | 5,378 |
| **Total New Rental Return** | 0 | 33,323 | 16,895 | 43,920 |
| | | | | |
| **Return on Invesment (ROI)** | 0 | 25.24% | 25.24% | 25.24% |

The "cash from equity" from the previous rental become the initial investment to calculate ROI on the new rental

## "New Rental" Section

The **"Returns on BOTH properties"** section combines the cash flow and returns from the current rental and the new rental. It'll show you what scenario maximizes cash flow and the total return.

| | #1: Keep It | #2A: Max Refi | #2B: Safe Refi | #3: Sell it |
|---|---|---|---|---|
| **Returns on BOTH properties** | | | | |
| Cumulative Cash Flow | $1,837 | $4,747 | $5,317 | $9,462 |
| Cumulative Returns (including cash flow) | $13,341 | $40,976 | $27,614 | $43,920 |

## "Returns on BOTH Properties" Section

# The Winner Is...

**Scenario #3** - Selling the rental, using a 1031 exchange and then buying a new rental property gave me the greatest cash flow AND the greatest overall return.

Scenario #3 will generate $9,462 a year in cash flow and about $44,000 in total returns the first year! That's a big step up from keeping the existing rental, which is returning $1,837 a year in cash flow and about $13,000 in total returns.

## The Final and Real Numbers

The numbers above are the real numbers I used to model my own decision on whether to sell the condo in Reno, NV to buy a fourplex in Denver, CO for $850,000. I did put 25% down and needed to bring additional cash to closing on top of the $174,000 from the sale of the Reno, NV condo. Below are screenshots of the Return on Investment Quadrant™ estimated returns from the detailed property analysis.

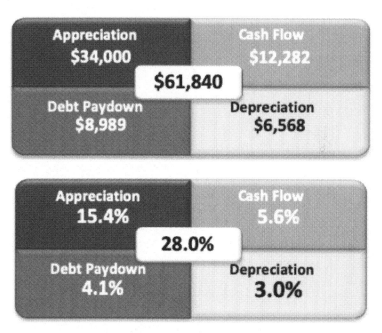

# Reno, NV condo vs. Denver, CO fourplex

|  | Reno, NV Condo | Denver, CO Fourplex |
|---|---|---|
| Cash Flow | $1,837 | $12,282 |
| True Cash Flow™ (=cash flow + Depreciation) | $2,354 | $18,850 |

The Reno, NV condo was generating a 6.9% return on equity. By selling the property—even with all the real estate transaction expenses to reposition the equity as a down payment—the capital is now earning me an estimated 28% ROI. I took the equity and converted it into an initial investment on a new rental property.

Here are some key principles to keep in mind as to why it's generating a greater return:

1. **More leverage** - The Reno, NV condo was at a 15.9% LTV, and the new fourplex is at a 75% LTV. Leverage gives you greater returns.

2. **Better rental** - The Reno, NV condo is a 3.58% cap, and the Denver fourplex is a 6.0% cap. I purchased a better rental property.

By selling and utilizing a 1031 exchange, I got the best of both worlds—more leverage and buying a better rental property while deferring my capital gains taxes.

# Conclusion

What's the highest and best use of the equity in your rental properties? It depends on the property and your goals. I'm in the accumulation phase of building my rental portfolio, so my goal is to acquire as many properties as possible. Plus, I'm not a fan of out-of-state investing, so moving the money from Reno, NV to Denver, CO is a better fit for my investing goals.

If you're nearing retirement, keeping the property and paying it off may be the best option for you. Then you're in the debt payoff phase (not the accumulation phase) of your real estate investing strategy.

Every year I'll put all my rental properties into the spreadsheet to calculate my return on equity and the opportunity costs of my equity. I'd advise you to do the same. One of my current projects is to build a real estate tracker spreadsheet to better track and calculate ROE and opportunity costs. If you're a client of mine, you'll get a copy once it's ready. We can sit down every year to review your portfolio and numbers.

At the time of writing this, I'm currently in the process of doing a rate and term only refinance on the fourplex to lower the interest rate from 5.25% to 3.75%, which will increase my cash flow by about $7,000 a year.

# Chapter 15

# House Hacking Interview - Ben & Alyson Einsphar

———————— o ————————

B en and Alyson are two of our clients who bought a great house hack property in Arvada in the Spring of 2019. We wanted to interview them because they have a great story and strategy for their house hacking method and are currently doing an Airbnb with their house hack.

Ben's interest in real estate investing started on a road trip with friends. They were casually talking about different ways to invest, and when real estate investing came up, Ben's friend suggested he listen to a BiggerPockets podcast, which he had started listening to on his drives to and from work. After a few episodes, he was hooked!

Alyson, on the other hand, admits she was skeptical at first about real estate investing. In 2015, when she and Ben first started dating, Ben was interested in investing in duplexes in Omaha, which sounded like "an absolute nightmare" to Alyson because of the tenant headaches, logistics and the fact that she prefers simplicity. She now admits that she should have appreciated Ben's financial readiness but, ultimately, still needed to do her own research to get on board fully.

After seeing Ben's passion, learning more about the numbers of everything and researching other female investors, Alyson decided to take a house hacking workshop that Joe and I held, and it helped clarify the process and handle hesitations Alyson had. She was able to see how real estate investing can be used as a tool for financial assistance and freedom in the future, and from that point, she caught the real estate bug as well.

Ben closed on his first property in December of 2017 in Omaha, Nebraska. About 6 months after closing on that property, he got wind of a job offer in Denver. By late 2018, Ben and Alyson had moved to Denver and became what Ben calls "accidental landlords" as a result of renting out his property in Omaha. They were living in a condo in Denver paying someone else's mortgage each month, which drove Ben bonkers.

They were ready to start house hacking in Denver!

Ben and Alyson were, at the time, living in a one-bedroom, one-bathroom condo for about $1,500 per month. Their goal was to get their monthly mortgage payment all-in (including principal, insurance, interest and taxes) to $1,000 or less.

So, they started the house hacking search. Their criteria, other than monthly payment, was that they didn't want any shared living space. For Alyson to feel comfortable, she did not want to share kitchen and bathroom space with potential Airbnb tenants each week. This really meant that they needed a place with totally separate living spaces and separate entrances.

Once they started to walk properties, there were really two options. They could look for places that they could renovate and make a few changes to make into separate units, or they could focus on places that were already set up to accommodate separate living spaces. Ultimately, they decided to focus on places that were already set up to work well as separate spaces because they didn't want to spend the time (three to six months) or money ($20k-$40k) to reconfigure the layout for separate living spaces. It was going to be difficult to come up with the money up front and it was then all lost in the property. Money that could potentially go towards the down payment of the next house hack. If they found a place that was already set up to house separate spaces, they could start their Airbnb rentals sooner and start collecting rents quickly.

Another reason it was important for Ben and Alyson to find a property that was really set up to hit the ground running was because they each had 9-5 jobs, which consumed most of their time. They didn't want to have to come home to more projects.

Initially, Ben and Alyson were actually thinking they might do long-term rentals instead of Airbnb. One issue with a long-term rental was that the upstairs unit did not have a washer and dryer, which was a deterrent for long-term renters. Also, when Ben started to look at the numbers for Airbnb and realized they could get between $95-$105 per night for Airbnb, it solidified the choice to go with Airbnb.

When they were actually looking for a property, which was spring of 2019, it was a very competitive market. After losing out on two offers, Ben and Alyson agreed to be a bit more aggressive on offers just to get their foot in the door before doing a deep dive into the numbers. It was more beneficial to make an offer and have it accepted than spending the time to look at the numbers in depth and run all scenarios, then running all scenarios up front and going back and forth so that, by the time they decided that a property worked, it was already under contract and no longer available.

This fits right in line with how we have described our process previously. It's better to make sure a property passes the "sniff test" and put an offer in, which costs little to no money. During the due diligence period of the contract, do the full and detailed underwriting. You then have time during the due diligence process to run every number and make sure it's the right fit.

After losing out on a few properties, Ben and Alyson were a little discouraged and had decided to take a break from looking for a while. Luckily, Alyson had secretly kept looking at the new listings each day and was able to find the slam dunk property they are currently in.

The property they are currently in is a four-bedroom, three-bathroom house. The main house is three-bedroom, two-bathroom, and the mother-in law-section is one-bedroom, one-bathroom. The key to this layout is that it is shaped like the letter "L". The main house being the long part of the "L" and the garage being the small part of the "L." The mother-in-law suite is above the garage and has a completely separate entrance. It's also nice because the "L" shape allows for more privacy for both Ben and Alyson as well as any Airbnb guests because they are not directly above or below the tenants.

To attract the highest rates for Airbnb, they decided to renovate the bathroom and kitchen in the mother-in-law suite portion of the property. The space did have new carpet and paint. After the renovations and furnishing the place (furniture, bedding, linens, plates, silverware, etc.), they spent about $5,000 over three months. They did all the work themselves.

When they started to list the property for short-term rental, they did a lot of research and actually started off pricing very low. They wanted to get a few tenants in there to build up great reviews to help with future bookings. Immediately, they started to fill their bookings. One of the biggest keys to their success was being on top of messages and questions that were coming in from potential tenants. Quick and clear communication is important.

Throughout the booking process, Ben and Alyson learned quickly that it was important to have templates ready to go (e.g. Welcome template, thank you for booking with us template, etc.) so that the communication was quick and efficient.

In the summer months, they were able to bring in $1,900-$2,100 per month, and occupancy rates were about 90%. The winter months were a bit slower and more competitive and brought in about $1,400-$1,700 per month. There were a lot of overlapping bookings (meaning check-out one guest; check-in next guest the same day), even during the week. To get the small gaps filled, they would drop the price by $10 for a Wednesday/Thursday gap.

Initially, Ben and Alyson were cleaning and "turning" the units themselves, but once they were able to recoup most of the costs from the renovations and pay off their Home Depot card, they started to use a cleaning service. Each clean is about $45 but you are able to add that fee to the rental through the Airbnb website. They added a $50 cleaning fee—the extra $5 is able to cover the consumable products like toilet paper, paper towels, etc.

Since COVID, things have changed, and cleaning standards have obviously become very important. After the cleaning service has "turned" the unit, Ben and Alyson will go in for one last check to make sure that every surface has been disinfected.

Another change due to COVID is that, if you advertise that you are able to host first responders in your rental, there is a requirement of 72 hours between each rental. The cleaning fees also went up as it was taking more time to clean each time.

All the money collected from Airbnb was pre-tax money, so Ben and Alyson would save about 28% of the monthly income as they knew they would have a big hit at the end of the year come tax time. The good news is that any work done involving the property was eligible as a tax write off (cleaning fees, landscaping, updates, etc.).

Luckily for Ben and Alyson, they had a tenant who had planned to stay in their Airbnb starting in March for 3 weeks. He actually extended his stay another week, which allowed Ben and Alyson to get through the brunt of the COVID lockdown with a tenant in place and allowed everyone to be safe and socially distance responsibly.

Come April, only 11 out of the 27 nights were booked. Occupancy rates dropped to about 41%, and nightly rates dropped to $35-$45 per night. Then, in May, they were able to get another longer-term renter who stayed all of May and into the first week of June. They actually put out listings on sites for traveling nurses and medium-term rentals as well just to play their odds and make sure all their options were available.

During the craziness and uncertainty of COVID, Alyson says that the Airbnb website was really great to work with. They were very on top of rules, regulations and communication to the hosts, and they offered great cancellation policies, giving 25% of the cancelation fees to the hosts.

As far as responsibilities, Ben and Alyson make a good team and agree to "divide and conquer." Alyson handles 90% of the communication with guests and bookings as well as communication with the Airbnb website if needed. Ben does all the updates and repairs if/when needed. They come together on financials and pricing. They have a system to make sure their checklist is done and choose to be more involved with the rentals than other hosts.

Coming into the house hacking and Airbnb scenario, Alyson had a few reservations. She was nervous about sharing space, if they would be able to book enough nights and all the unknowns of tenants. *Will they smoke in the unit? Will they leave a candle burning? How do we remove someone if they end up being a complete nightmare?* A year later, what Alyson has learned is that most people are great! They have met some amazing people, and the majority of the guests are wonderful. As far as having separate space, it's not too different than living in an apartment or condo complex—it's like they are your neighbors. While they have had very few nightmare guests, if there is a problem, it's great to be able to rely on Airbnb to help intervene and solve those issues. Overall, Alyson didn't think she would enjoy it as much as she does and has been pleasantly surprised and really enjoys the process.

Ben reiterates that what once was foreign and started as something very much outside of their comfort zone, is now part of their "norm." It's process they have grown to enjoy and is an investment where the benefits far outweigh the sacrifices.

They are also supplementing their mortgage payments with the long-term rent they collect by renting a room in their part of the house to Alyson's sister. They charge her $700 per month to help offset any expenses they have, which is slightly under market rent. It's a great win-win for everyone. They don't mind sharing this space because it's family.

Coincidentally, by living with Ben and Alyson, and by just having conversations with guests who stay in the Airbnb, Alyson's sister was actually offered a job by one of the guests. She now works remotely for him!

As far as investing goals for 2020, Ben and Alyson want to update the Airbnb exterior and be as conservative as possible with their money so they are in a good financial position for 2021 to get into their next house hack.

Once Ben and Alyson find their next house hack, they can either turn the current house into a long-term rental with a separate long-term rental for the mother-in-law suite, or they can work with someone who wants to rent out part of the house long-term and continue the Airbnb aspect with the other part of the house. The laws in Arvada state that, to have an Airbnb, it must be your permanent residence. This means that once Ben and Alyson move out, they can no longer run the Airbnb officially. They could, however, work out an agreement with the long-term renter to run the Airbnb because the house is the tenant's primary residence.

If they choose to do the longer-term rental, they think they can conservatively get about $1,100-$1,200 per month for the mother-in-law suite and about $2,100 for the main house. There are several options, you just have to get creative.

As far as the next house hack, they will look for a similar set up where they do not have to share space. They will also try to have Alyson's sister move with them and continue to rent a room in their new place. They love Arvada so will look to stay in the same area. Ideally, Ben would like to continue this strategy until they have gained financial freedom, but, realistically, he can see them doing it at least two or three more times—or until their family situation changes, or Alyson doesn't want to continue house hacking.

Alyson's advice when considering house hacking is to know your deal-breakers and what you're not willing to sacrifice. Stick to that and find a property that works within your expectations, otherwise you will not be happy.

Ben's advice is to make sure you have the discipline and grit to make it work. It won't always be easy, but it will be worth it if you stick to it. It's easy to come up with excuses like, "I don't have the time," or, "I don't have money." In reality, you have time for anything you want to make time for.

House hacking and teaching others has become a passion for Ben. At the time of this writing, Ben and I are working on co-hosting house hacking masterminds. Initially they'll be virtual meetings and eventually transition to in-person masterminds as COVID allows.

If you have more questions about Ben and Alyson's house hack, how to Airbnb, or just want to pick their brain, please reach to Ben via email at agrotheer25@gmail.com.

# Chapter 16

# House Hacking Interview - Austin Allan

———————○———————

Austin Allan is a client of ours who bought his first house hack recently and decided to do a room by room house hack in Aurora.

Like a lot of people, Austin had been thinking about real estate investing for a while but wasn't sure of the best way to get started. He started reading and doing a lot of self-education. I met Austin in 2017, and he says that the information he got from our team was what made him start thinking differently about real estate and see how it can be an option, even for someone who isn't necessarily wealthy (or not wealthy yet).

Austin claims that there wasn't one book or one person that really gave him that "ah-ha" moment, but since high school and working at an affluent country club atmosphere, he saw people around him gaining wealth and status with real estate.

As far as choosing an investment path that is right for him, Austin felt that house hacking was a great fit because it allowed him to execute his investing goals relatively quickly as well as provided creative financing and multiple options on how to be successful through the method of house hacking.

As an example, the house hacking method allowed Austin to buy a house with a partner and get it set up for a room by room rental for

$22,000 total. It's rare to find another investment opportunity with such a low barrier to entry. He and his partner were able to get educated by listening to our podcasts and webinars, so they felt comfortable to make the house hack purchase quickly. If they had gone on their own, they would not have been able to buy the house as quickly and start gaining the real estate benefits because they would still be saving for the down payment.

It's not always easy to find a good business partner. In Austin's case, he and his partner have known each other since high school, they have worked together on car projects in the past, and while their minds work and think differently, they complement each other, which allows for a good decision-making team. It's important when forming a partnership that you have established trust and a history of working together so you know what you're in for.

Austin thrives in the areas of marketing and management; his partner is better at operations and structure. All these traits of working together lead to a good partnership. Austin and his partner are able to communicate well and bounce ideas off of each other to make quick yet educated decisions, which will help them now and in the future.

The house that we helped Austin and his business partner buy was a 5-bedroom, 2-bathroom house in north Aurora, near the Anschutz Medical Campus. When they first started their house search, they were looking on the west side of town near Lakewood but felt that the houses they were finding were needing more work to get them updated and rentable than Austin was willing to put in. Neither Austin nor his business partner had the time to do the updates. Plus, they didn't have a budget to renovate everything. So, they decided to start looking near the Anschutz Medical Campus.

There was and still is a lot of construction going on in that area for housing, shops, restaurants and entertainment, which is a great sign for appreciation. The area is also a great "commuter hub." It's close to 225, I-25, I-70 and DIA, and is only eight miles from downtown Denver. They were able to find a house that was in good shape and essential turnkey.

Another thing that Austin learned was that room by room rents in Aurora are surprisingly very similar to Denver rent. Initially, they were thinking they could rent to the nursing students who were all needing to be close to the medical campus. With the timing of the purchase, they missed the wave of nursing students but were pleasantly surprised that they still had lots of demand for the room rentals.

After closing on the house, Austin's first step was to get great pictures of the place and get it furnished because all he moved in with were his belongings and a couch. Austin and his business partner debated about furnishing the place or letting tenants bring their own things into the rental but found out quickly that most of the people looking for the room rentals didn't have much of anything, so it was an easy decision to furnish the place.

This coincided with our house hacking coach, Jeff White's, advice in his chapter that furnishing the place makes the move in/out easier. In short, control everything you can control!

Austin uses Cozy.co for prospective tenants to submit applications, run background checks and pay rent. It makes it easy for you as a landlord, easy for the tenant and gives confidence to both parties that there is a system in place. By using Cozy.co, you're not liable for any sensitive information like a social security number.

As far as marketing the property, Austin started with the basic Facebook Marketplace and Craig's List posts but didn't get much traction. He did some research and found better success once he started to join the niche Facebook groups, like "Anschutz Subletting" and "Aurora Rental." Austin says he was spending about 1-2 hours a day on Facebook not only advertising his property but also reading the posts and reaching out to individuals directly if he thought his rental would be a fit with what they were looking for. So, he was doing sales outreach while also marketing.

Once Austin connected with someone who wanted more information on the place, he would private message them with the specifics on the house and room that was available. If the person liked that info, they would set up a time to see the house/room and possibly meet the other roommates. If the house was going to be a fit and Austin got a good feeling from them after meeting and talking about the living arrangements, the potential renters were instructed to fill out an application online. Austin mentions that it was important to him that each renter followed the same steps so there was no question of discrimination and he could get a better idea of the person based on if they got pushback from any of the steps or not. It also shows how serious the person to rent. Altogether, Austin had about seven people come to the house, which resulted in three tenants signing leases.

Austin also gives good advice and cautions that with these house hack situations, you need to be a bit more picky with renters because you are going to have to live with these people and see them every day when you come home. You don't want it to be miserable, so it's important that you get a good feeling about their personality and vibe during the initial interview or walk-through.

As we mentioned before, the house has five bedrooms, two bathrooms, and there are currently four roommates (Austin included). The fifth bedroom is smaller and renting it would mean that three people would need to share a smaller bathroom instead of just two people sharing. Initially, Austin didn't like the idea of three people sharing a small bathroom and was worried about the cleanliness of everyone. Also, Austin switched jobs recently and is working from home, so the small bedroom has been turned into an office. Even though the space is being used, after living there for a couple months and seeing how easily two tidy people can easily share a small bathroom, Austin is now more open to renting out the fifth bedroom and focusing on maximizing rents.

Austin knows that rent in Denver is not cheap. His goal is to provide everyone in the house with reasonable rent and a comfortable living environment. He does this by having good communication, setting clear expectations and leading by example, especially when it comes to cleaning up after himself.

Currently, two of the rooms are renting for $800/month each, and one is rented for $750/month. House Wi-Fi and all utilities are included in the rent. If Austin wanted to rent out one floor (top or bottom), he thought he could rent it for about $1200-$1500/month.

Now that Austin has his rooms rented and the process is running smoothly after a couple of months, we wanted to ask him if there was anything that surprised him about the process, or if there was anything that he hadn't expected going into this project. Austin says that the only thing that really surprised him was the amount of capital they needed to get everything up and going. They needed to fix an electrical issue under the sink (listen to the podcast to hear about how Austin was almost electrocuted!), blinds for the windows, furniture and other minor things that you just don't think about when you buy the place but end up causing you to take 15 Home Depot trips, costing you an extra $1,000. The good thing in Austin's situation is that $1,000 is actually only $500 per person of capital. For the next house hack, he will know to put a little more money in the bank for these minor things to get going.

So, while the first house hack has been an adventure, Austin has learned a ton and is now more prepared to be even more efficient with the next one. Even with all the frustrations and taking a new job with a pay cut, Austin is able to live comfortably with a 50% savings rate. He's sold on the house hacking method 100% and can't wait for the next one.

Austin says, "You obviously have to deal with living with people, which isn't always easy," but the sooner you can get into a house hack, the better off you'll be. Once you see the numbers and savings, it's worth the sacrifice. If you are worried about the capital, find a partner who wants to get into it as well. It's better to be 50% of a deal than 0% of a deal.

Austin enjoys networking and helping others navigate their house hack. You can connect with him at Austin.allan87@gmail.com.

# Chapter 17

# House Hacking in Colorado Springs

———————◦———————

While writing this book, a great opportunity popped up to partner with an agent in Colorado Springs. Her name is Jenny Bayless. She's an active investor in the Springs and a CPA turned investor-friendly Realtor. Long story short, we had just enough time to add a chapter on Colorado Springs to this book to highlight some of the differences. If you're interested in the Springs market, make sure you keep an eye on our podcast and email list as Jenny and I will be doing a deep dive into the market!

If you want to connect with Jenny to ask her questions or explore the Colorado Springs market, just go to www.DenverInvestmentRealEstate.com/consult.

Here's Jenny's contribution:

Just an hour south of Denver, Colorado Springs presents an amazing opportunity to house hack your way to growing your wealth through rental properties. Colorado Springs is home to multiple military bases, large tech employers, and many beautiful natural landmarks such as Pike's Peak and Garden of the Gods—all of which contribute to a healthy and strong economy. It is quickly becoming a city to watch as it consistently places high on many lists. For example, US News and World Report ranked Colorado Springs as the #1 Most Desirable Place to Live in 2018, and Realtor.com rated it as #5 Hottest Housing

Markets in 2019. Not to mention—this might come as a surprise to the Denverites reading this—but Colorado Springs' growth rate in home values was almost double that of Denver's from 2019 to 2020, at 7%! Furthermore, Colorado Springs' median sales price for single-family homes was $360,000 in June 2020, which many house hackers may find to be a more affordable entry point.

# What's the Best Location in Colorado Springs?

What is the best area to house hack in Colorado Springs? As the rest of this book has echoed: it depends!

Colorado Springs offers the same house hacking options and strategies as Denver. Where in the city you should focus your search will depend on what your investment goals and preferences are. This section highlights house hacking in Colorado Springs, but there are plenty of other opportunities in the surrounding metro area such as Woodland Park, Peyton, Falcon, Monument, Fountain, etc. These areas are not covered in this book. Additionally, it is important to work with your lender as discussed previously because the conforming loan limit is different for El Paso County than for Denver and surrounding counties.

The following suggestions are merely a starting point using generalized information for your house hacking journey in Colorado Springs. The strategies are not exclusive to the areas and options below, but they are a good place to begin your search. For instance, if a client wants to live in a certain part of town, we would suggest the most optimized house hack strategy based on location. Conversely, if the client had a particular strategy in mind, we'd share the areas of town with the most opportunity to successfully perform that house hack strategy.

# Central and Southeast Colorado Springs

Generally speaking, the central and southeast regions, as well as some parts of the airport area of Colorado Springs, lend themselves best to the room by room strategy of house hacking. The reasons are two-fold: first, the price-to-rent ratio purely based on bedroom count is better than most other parts of Colorado Springs, and second, with the homes being older, there is usually room to better utilize space. I have noticed that, in this area of Colorado Springs, there are a lot of homes with basements or rooms that are not being efficiently utilized.

A simple yet effective strategy for increasing value and cash flow is the addition of a bedroom and bathroom. This method does not have to be complicated, or increase the footprint of the home through an addition or anything difficult and cost-prohibitive, rather a house hacker can simply look for poorly utilized existing space in a home. By closing off a room or converting a powder room into a full bath, you can greatly increase the value of the property as well as its rental potential for just a few thousand dollars. For example, I have one rental property in southeast Colorado Springs that was purchased as a 3 bed/1.5 bath for $165,000. The main reason I bought this property was because I saw in the basement there was a rec room tucked away next to a half bath (which was conveniently located next to the utility closet). By spending a few thousand dollars to convert the rec room into a bedroom (by adding a wall, door and closet—it already had an egress window) and the half bath into a three-quarter, the home was re-appraised at $240,000 about one year after purchase. I am not saying that by adding a bed and a bath you will realize $75,000 in added value, but this is an option to explore, and your real estate agent can help you determine if there is room in the comps to utilize this method to increase value.

By employing this strategy, the house hacker has a lot of options! They can stick to the room by room method and rent out the new additional bedroom for supplemental monthly income. This also means that, once the house hacker moves out of the property, they can command higher rents for a 4-bed vs. a 3-bed, even if they rent by the house and not by the room. Also, the house hacker could potentially use one of the return on equity analyses discussed in this book to potentially re-deploy the increased equity created.

# Westside and Downtown

The Westside, or more specifically, Old Colorado City and parts of downtown/Memorial Park areas would best lend themselves to multi-family and Airbnb house hacking options. In this part of town, you are more likely to find R-2 or R-4 zoning. What this means is that certain properties are zoned for duplex or multi-family units (R-2 allows for 2 units), which allows the house hacker to legally subdivide existing properties, or to live in one unit and rent the other unit(s) of a property that has already been subdivided.

Not to mention, this part of town is generally a tourism hot spot as it is just a quick drive to Pike's Peak, Garden of the Gods, and local shops and restaurants. This can potentially lend itself to an Airbnb option while living in the property. It is important to understand that Colorado Springs recently underwent many legislative changes related to short-term rental housing as of late 2019, and could further evolve at any time. What I always offer as a suggestion to investors is to underwrite a deal NOT using Airbnb as a revenue source (only look at long-term rental rates), but if the laws allow for it, it is a good option to offer the unit as an Airbnb if currently authorized. In any event, it is best to contact your attorney to fully understand the short-term rental laws.

# Northern Colorado Springs

If you drive down the Powers Corridor, you will see new construction homes at every turn. This part of town is not only very close to Peterson Air Force Base and many tech employers, but it is quickly becoming an alternative location to live for those who commute to Denver but want a more affordable cost of living and purchase price of homes. Not to mention, in general, Colorado Springs is seeing a higher appreciation rate than Denver this past year.

I mentioned previously that the room by room strategy works better in central and southeast Colorado Springs in comparison to northern Colorado Springs due to the price-to-rent ratio and ability to force equity by adding bedrooms. However, this does not mean that northern Colorado Springs does not allow for a house hack opportunity in general. The room by room strategy would still allow the house hacker to offset their mortgage and living expenses. An Additional benefit to purchasing a home in this area is that the homes tend to be new builds or only a few years old, which would mean that the investor could assume lower maintenance costs in the initial years of owning the home. Further, the houses tend to be larger in this area. If the investor values more personal space (such as larger bedrooms) but still wants to optimize revenue by renting by the room, these locations could offer this balance. Upon moving out of the home, the investor may typically realize break-even cash flow if converted to a single-family home rental, but as this book highlights, there are other factors (tax benefits, appreciation, debt paydown) that will contribute towards a positive return on investment.

These houses also would allow for a great opportunity for a mother-in-law suite house hack. The houses are typically large in size (3,000 sq. ft+), which would allow a house hacker more personal space on the upper level of the house while possibly outfitting the basement to utilize a multigenerational house hack.

# Colorado Springs House Hack Example

Let's walk through an example house hack located in central Colorado Springs near downtown. This example property was found on the Pike's Peak MLS (PPMLS) in Q3 of 2020, and the property already has a kitchenette and second entrance, lending itself to being an easy conversion into a second living space. It is zoned appropriately at R-4 (meaning multi-family residential is authorized) to allow for a two-family set-up. In this case, we have budgeted for $10,000 to properly convert the home from a 3/2, to a 2/1 and 1/1 duplex.

Let's also assume the house hacker in this case does not wish to fully optimize their revenue and would prefer to live in the larger unit of this property for personal comfort and preference. While living in the property, the house hacker would have about $900 in rent from the smaller unit, plus a portion of utilities to go towards offsetting their mortgage and expenses. At the time this book was written, it is reasonable to assume a 3.00% interest rate on an owner-occupied property, so we are looking at a mortgage principal and interest payment of $1,262 and estimated escrow for insurance and taxes of $220 per month. Excluding any additional expenses (such as utilities and landscaping) and repairs, our house hacker is now living for just shy of $600 a month, while owning a $315,000+ asset. Not bad! To optimize even further, the house hacker in this case could very easily rent the second bedroom in their 2/1 unit for $500 a month, reducing their total portion of the mortgage to about $100.

Let's see what the house hacker could realize after Nomading™ out of the property:

| Property Address | COS House Hack |
|---|---|
| Number of Units | 2 |
| Initial Occupancy Status | Investment Property |

| Down Payment Percentage | 5% |
|---|---|

| Type of Mortgage Insurance | Monthly Paid |
|---|---|

| Purchase Price | $ | 315,000 |
|---|---|---|
| Acquisition Costs | $ | 5,000 |
| Loan Costs | $ | 1,540 |
| Down Payment | $ | 15,750 |
| Mortgage Balance | $ | 299,250 |
| Seller Credits | $ | - |
| Initial Repair Costs | $ | 10,000 |
| Total Initial Investment | $ | 32,290 |

| Mortgage Interest Rate | 3.000% |
|---|---|
| Mortgage Term (years) | 30 |

### MONTHLY Rental Income Per Unit

| Unit #1 | $ | 1,100 |
|---|---|---|
| Unit #2 | $ | 900 |
| Unit #3 | | |
| Unit #4 | | |
| Total Rental Income | $ | 2,000 |

| | |
|---|---|
| **Vacancy Factor** | 3% |
| **Annual Rent Increase** | 3% |
| **Annual Appreciation Rate** | 5% |
| **Effective Tax Rate** | 25% |

## Monthly Operating Expenses

| | |
|---|---|
| **Do you pay for property management?** | No |
| **Monthly Reserves for Maintenance - Percentage** | 8.0% |
| **Is there an HOA** | No |

## Additional Annual Expenses

| | | |
|---|---|---|
| **Annual Real Estate Taxes** | $ | 1,105 |
| **Annual Property Insurance** | $ | 1,500 |
| **Utilities (If paid by owner)** | | |
| **- Water and Sewer** | | |
| **- Trash** | $ | - |
| **- Electric** | | |
| **Landscaping** | $ | 500.00 |

At the time of writing this book, the rents budgeted are conservative, considering the proximity to downtown. Each unit could easily get $100-150 more a month than budgeted. Further, we assumed the house hacker in this case doesn't mind managing the property themselves. For reference, Colorado Springs has recently seen a 7% annual appreciation rate on home values and a 4% rent appreciation rate, in which we have conservatively underwritten 5% and 3% respectively.

| Net Operating Income | $ | 18,255 | | | | | | |
|---|---|---|---|---|---|---|---|---|
| Less: Annual Mortgage Payments | $ | (15,140) | $299,250 | @ | 3.000% | = | $1,261.65 | per month |
| Less: Annual Mortgage Payments | $ | (1,287) | Estimated Mortgage Insurance | | = | | $107 | per month |
| **Annual Cash Flow Before Taxes** | **$** | **1,828** | | | | | | |

| | *1st Year Returns* | | | | | | |
|---|---|---|---|---|---|---|---|
| **Cash-on-Cash Rate of Return** | **5.7%** | $1,828 | ÷ | $32,290 | = | 6% | |
| **CAP Rate** | **5.6%** | $18,255 | ÷ | $325,000 | = | 5.6% | |
| **GRM - Gross Rent Multiplier** | **162.5** | $325,000 | ÷ | $2,000 | = | 162.5 | |

**1st Year Return On Investment Quadrant™ (ROIQ)**

| Appreciation 48.8% | Cash Flow 5.7% | | Appreciation $15,750 | Cash Flow $1,828 |
|---|---|---|---|---|
| **81.3%** | | | **$26,260** | |
| Debt Paydown 19.3% | Depreciation 7.5% | | Debt Paydown $6,248 | Depreciation $2,434 |

**Return On Investment Quadrant™ is a trademark of Real Estate Financial Planner LLC

This property is ideal for a house-hack-to-Nomad™ opportunity. With only a 5% down conventional loan, there would also be some upfront costs to partition off the separate living areas and to add to the already existing kitchenette. Further, we assessed an 8% yearly repair/maintenance budget for this property, which is very conservative since the home has recently been fully remodeled. Assuming a self-managed approach both during the house hack and upon Nomading™, this is a solid deal.

# Chapter 18

# Working With Us

W e hope this book gave you the technical knowledge needed for your house hacking journey. If you're interested in working with us, please reach out. We're all happy to discuss your situation and see how we can help you out.

**Chris Lopez is an Investor-friendly agen**t at Your Castle Real Estate. He helps investors build a rental portfolio through house hacking and buying traditional rental properties. He also helps investors create a real estate retirement plan to target a monthly cash flow in retirement. Chris is also an investor and is currently doing a multigenerational family house hack. You can reach Chris at 303-548-0846 or Chris@DenverInvestmentRealEstate.com

**Joe Massey is a Senior Loan Officer and Branch Manager at Castle & Cooke Mortgage.**

Joe helps house hackers, investors and homebuyers with getting the best permanent financing in place based on their situation and the property. Joe is an active investor. You can reach Joe at 303-809-7769 or jmassey@castlecookemortgage.com

**Jeff White is a house hacking coach** who helps investors with maximizing their returns and stabilizing their properties. He's an active house hacker who is using this investing method to achieve financial independence. You can reach Jeff at 720-951-6868 or thehousehackingcoach@gmail.com.

If you have any questions, do not hesitate to reach out to us. We're always happy to chat about investing.